ED & IVET

THE TRUE STORY
OF A WORLD WAR II POW ROMANCE

WILLIAM BACON

B&H Bennett & Hastings Publishing

© 2010 William Bacon

All rights reserved. No part of this book may be reproduced or transmitted in any form by any means, electronic or mechanical, including photocopying and recording, or by any information storage and retrieval system, except as may be expressly permitted by the 1976 Copyright Act or the publisher. Requests for permission should be made in writing to: Bennett & Hastings Publishing, c/o the address posted at www.bennetthastings.com.

Photographs from the personal collection of the author unless otherwise noted.

Special thanks to George Sidline and Barbara Thomas for their kind permission to quote works under copyright to them, and to Naila Woodruff for permission to quote from her husband's unpublished diary.

Edited by Jill Kelly, PhD (www.jillkellyeditor.com)

ISBN: 978-1-934733-64-6, First Edition.

Library of Congress Control Number: 2010941320

This book is dedicated to my nieces and nephews.

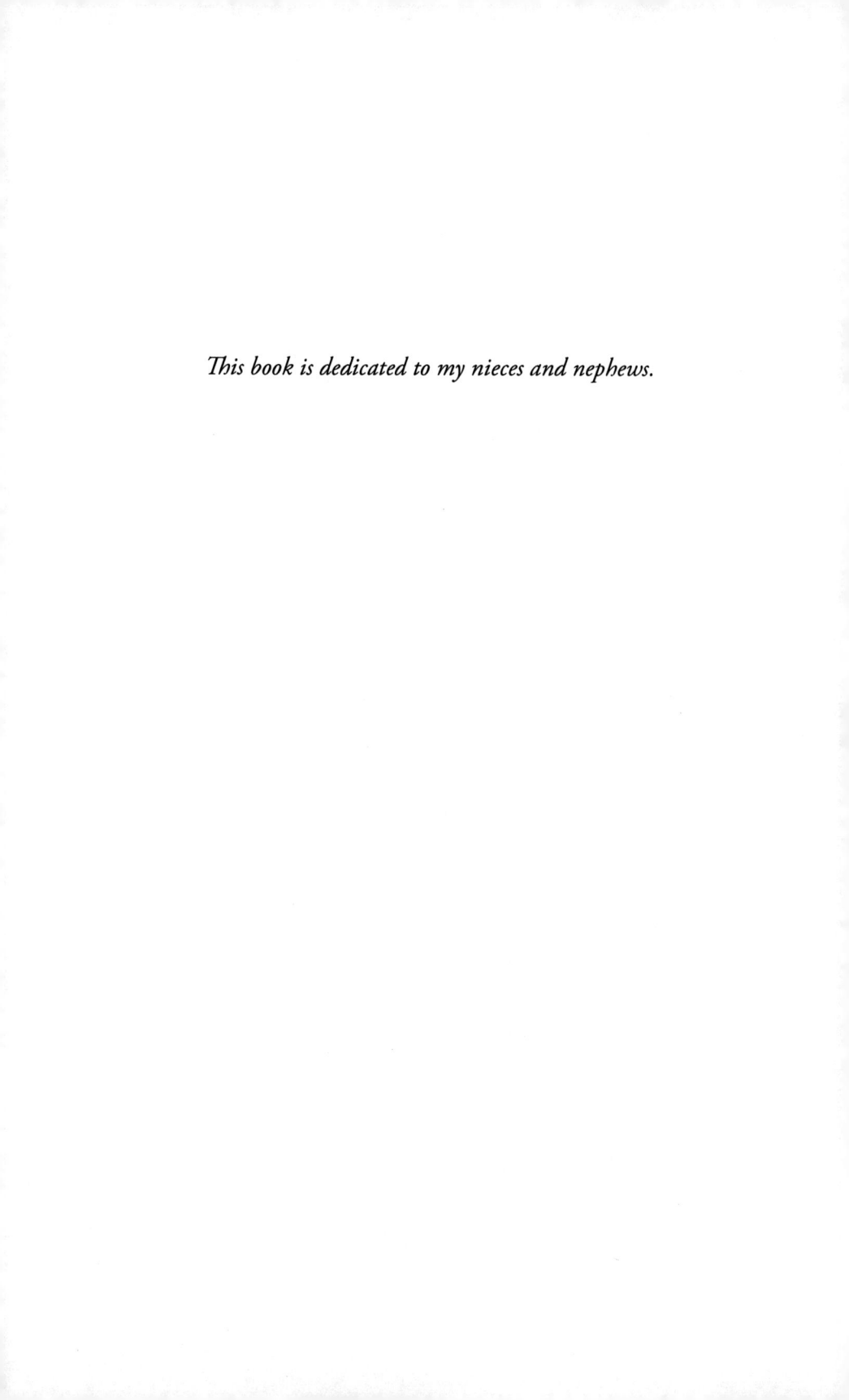

Contents

Dedication

Acknowledgements vii

Introduction ix

Part One: Ancestry 13
Ivet's Family Tree: East European Tatars 15
Ed's Family Tree: New England Bacons 23

Part Two: My Parents' Early Years 31
Ed's Early Years: "Edd" 33
Ivet's Early Years: "Effie" 43

Part Three: Ed's Capture 53
1941: Ed Ventures to Guam 55
Japanese Attack: Ed Is Captured 61
Zentsuji: Ed's First Internment 67
Seaman's Mission: Ed's Second Internment 73
Marks House: Ed's Third Internment 79
1943: Diaries and Letters 87

Part Four: Romance 93
Ed and Ivet Meet 95
Another Romance: Naila and Woody 103

Part Five: The Heart of War 107

1944: Bitter Winter and Starvation 109

Futatabi: Ed's Fourth Internment 115

Angel of Mercy: Ivet Takes Action 119

The Stickel-Bacon-Woodruff Company 125

St. Patrick's Day Bombing 131

Naila and Woody Caught 139

Air Raids and a Silver Ring 143

Love Escapes the Ruins 149

Part Six: Freedom 153

War Ends: Ed Meets Safa 155

Ed and Ivet Marry 163

Complications in the Philippines 169

Journey Home 173

Epilogue 181

Acknowledgements

Several people are deserving of special thanks. My Uncle Rashid for his wit and keen memory and my late Uncle Sam for his captivating tales and sense of humor. My Aunt Farida for revealing new sides to a familiar story and my Aunt Naila for sharing her remarkable memories and her late husband's diary with me.

My late Aunt Marge for filling in the gaps of my father's childhood and offering insights into what led to his journey. And my distant cousin Robert Dorsey, former Angelica Town Historian, for photos and stories that will surprise my family.

Other historians have been invaluable as well. Thanks to Irek Bikkinin, Tatar historian and philologist, for his scholarship and countless replies from Saransk; Pavlo Batukov, who translated scores of my grandfather's Russian documents; and the late Roger Mansell, whose extensive POW research led me directly to my father's fellow POWs and other contemporaries of the war.

Special thanks to George Sidline, who not only shared his personal stories of the war but also introduced me to my editor. And to Dwight R. Rider, who generously offered a review of this book.

I am also indebted to those who helped produce this work. My editor, Jill Kelly, who was understanding, professional, and accessible. Publisher Celeste Bennett for her endurance and patience. And for my reader-support team, Peggy Gaynor and Lynda Stoye, who often had the last words of advice.

Finally, to my mother and father who never ceased to love each other and who lived out this amazing story that I merely put to print.

Introduction

Shakespeare once wrote that *all the world's a stage, and all the men and women merely players ... and one man in his lifetime plays many parts.* Sometimes the most compelling stories are from those people whose scripts have changed dramatically.

I was reminded of this recently while watching a 1945 home movie of my parents who were outside an upscale San Francisco apartment building on a sunny day. Waving and gesturing to the camera, they were all smiles. My mother, in particular, was kissing and hugging everyone—my father, my aunt, my grandmother. My parents were so young, so animated, so full of joy and all groomed in sophisticated 1940s fashions. As I sat watching the movie, I couldn't help thinking that no one would have guessed that only months prior to this, all these people were enduring a kind of hell we can only imagine.

My parents were Ed and Ivet Bacon. Many in our family remember them simply as Mom and Popi. Ed and Ivet came from opposite ends of the world. He was the son of a physician and grew up in the Midwest plains of Colorado. She was born in Japan, the daughter of Moslem Tatars who'd emigrated from Russia.

There is an old saying that *East is east and West is west and never the twain shall meet.* But there is another saying that *there is an exception to every rule.*

Ed and Ivet met secretly during World War II while my father was a prisoner of war in Japan. Their story was a script challenged by prison fences, cultural mores, and religious obstacles as well as the never-ending threat of exposure. During the height of the war, they faced relentless night air raids, incendiary bombs, and starvation—all in a country that was, culturally, foreign to both of them. This is the tale of a very unlikely love story.

As my brothers and sisters and I grew older, we learned more of my parents' early romance. The stage then was Sunday night dinners in our benign San Francisco suburb of Burlingame during the 1960s and 1970s. There was always a reason to retell my parents' story whether it was for one of my sisters' new boyfriends, a visiting relative, or a neighbor joining us for dinner. The odds of my parents' meeting was so remote and the setting so foreign to our quiet suburban life that hearing the events never grew tiresome. We were also fortunate to have my aunts and uncles on both sides of the family living close by—an impressive cast of characters who were a constant reminder of this exotic marriage of two worlds.

In addition to all the storytelling, there were the contents of my father's bronze file-safe. The safe was a small tin box, twelve inches tall with locks, drawers, and folders. It was full of urgent telegrams, stamped envelopes, old letters and photos, foreign coins and currency, birth certificates, news clippings, old military parchments, membership cards, badges, seals and, last but not least, my father's POW diary. My god, I used to think, they kept everything. Often, by the end of a Sunday night dinner, the contents of the entire box were spread over the dining table as we sat spellbound, exploring the remnants of a distant time and place in my parents' lives.

Later, while I was away at college, I developed a growing interest in journalism. At the same time, the idea of chronicling this love story was growing more and more compelling to me. Consequently, I began collecting taped and written memories that my parents had of the war and of their meeting. Sometimes I had to trick them. Once I told my mother that answering a set of questions I sent her was part of a class project. She fell for it. It remains the only handwritten account of her experiences before, during, and after the war. I also captured my uncles' stories on tape. I knew talks with them always resulted in humorous reminiscences. So during one visit, I smuggled in a pocket recorder. After a few glasses of wine, I casually pulled out the recorder and set it on the dining table.

Now, many years later, while my parents have passed away, I continue to pester my aunts and uncles with phone calls. The calls pay off. Many of the details in this book are the result of recent conversations. In addition, just years ago I discovered another diary. My late Uncle Woody was a POW in the same camp with my father. His wife, my Aunt Naila, offered to let me read the diary. Needless to say, Uncle Woody's diary added new dimensions to this distant romance.

Collecting and compiling these stories invariably led me into my family's genealogy. Understanding where Ed and Ivet came from magnified not only what is unusual about their romance but, ironically, what is often common in life. That life endures even after tragedy. Reports on hurricanes almost always focus on the destructive side of weather. Rarely are we reminded that hurricanes also cool the earth, replenish wetland habitats with overflow sediments, and cleanse coastal forests. Likewise, war has varying consequences. War is destructive; it uproots people. War disturbs political climates. Empires rise and fall. But war, like hurricanes, can also leave new beginnings in its wake.

The melancholy character in Shakespeare's play goes on to list seven stages in a man's life, ultimately ending *sans teeth, sans eyes, sans taste, sans everything*. I like to think there is another stage. Reminiscence. The final appreciation of another's life. A professor once defined reminiscence as "adding to remembering." *Ed & Ivet* is an attempt to quilt my parents' ancestry, letters, telegrams, and contemporary history along with new eye-witness accounts of that Sunday night story of how a captured American Episcopalian son of a doctor met a young Turkish Moslem girl in the hills of Kobe, Japan during World War II.

Ed and Ivet passed away in 1998 and 1999, respectively. Not soon after I held my brother's newborn granddaughter Kayla in my arms and thought to myself, she will never hear Ed and Ivet tell their story. I worried the story would fade away as she grew older—unless someone wrote it down. And so, to Kayla and all my other nieces and nephews past, present, and future: here is the story of Mom and Popi.

For my family, I offer this for posterity and as a tribute to two cherished souls who were the essence of home and love, family and comfort and who left for us a cherished stage of memories. For others who might be curious, this is a story that reminds us that those of distant worlds can fall in love with each other and that sometimes the greatest rewards in life are found during the worst of times.

PART ONE: ANCESTRY

Ivet's Family Tree:
East European Tatars

AKCHURIN

Ed and Ivet came from opposite ends of the world. It is in large part why their meeting is so unusual. Their story begins with an introduction to Ivet's side of the family.

It was 1918 and the cities and villages of Russia were turning red in more ways than one. Uprisings, revolts, and massacres in the tens of thousands left a bloody landscape, the scope of which Russia had never seen before as the Red Terror followed the White Terror in a ravaging civil war.

My grandfather witnessed this from all too close at hand and, no doubt, eventually walked through the wheat fields of his family's 90 acres[1] with bated breath, trying to feel something of the grain with his palms outstretched as he paced in a daze. But in this climate he could find no

---

[1] Bikkinin, I. Zemski *Agricultural All-Russian Census of 1917*, p. 9

comfort in the familiar ground he walked on. When you have watched your father murdered in front of your very eyes, what is there left to feel?

My grandfather was born Muhamedsafa Çerulla Akchurin in 1894 in the village of Ust Rahkmanovka, 200 miles southeast of Moscow. He was known to us grandkids as "Baba" and as "Safa" to the adults. Safa was an educated Mishar Tatar. Mishar Tatars are found in western Russian and they originate from Slavic and northern European peoples, especially those from southern Finland[2]. Mishars have been described as "turkicized Eastern Finns[3]" since their native *Tatarça* is considered a Turkic language. Safa was also a Sunni Moslem, and one of nine sons born of Çerulla and Halimzah Akchurin. His father was a wealthy landowner who, among other things, raised horses for the Czar's army as well as being outspoken and active in politics—a perfect candidate for the growing resentment of emerging Bolsheviks in 19th-century Russia.

While Lenin was recovering from an assassination attempt, he sent chilling telegrams blatantly urging "mass terror." One telegram singled out "landowners in Penza" with gruesome instructions:

> *Comrades!... You must make an example of these people. Hang (I mean hang them publicly so that people see it) at least 100 kulaks, rich bastards and known bloodsuckers. Publish their names and seize their grain.*[4]

Penza was just 75 miles from my grandfather's village where the terror of his youth set the stage for his nightmares as his father—that wealthy, political, Moslem peasant—was burned at the stake by raging Bolshevik revolutionaries.

This tragedy in my grandfather's life was a story I first heard as a teenager. My mother translated as my grandmother recalled the incident

---

[2] Bikkinin, I. *The Tatar Gazette*, 1999.
[3] www.turkiye.net/sota/tatarfaq.html; Minahan, J. *Encyclopedia of Stateless Nations: Ethnic and National Groups around the World: Vol. IV S-Z.*, Westport, CT: Greenwood Press, pp. 1856-1859.
[4] Werth, N., et al. (1999). *The Black Book of Communism: Crimes, Terror, Repression.* Cambridge, MA: Harvard University Press.

in her native tongue. Years later, I questioned other relatives about my great-grandfather's death.

"When I was a child, I remember Pop [Safa] often crying out from nightmares," my uncle Rashid said.

Also recalling her father's nightmares, my aunt Farida added, "We were young. We didn't want to make things harder for Dad by asking him questions as to why he was crying."

"It wasn't until later we were told that Safa was forced to watch his father's death, which is what his nightmares were all about," my mother explained.

Safa was 24 at the time of the Revolution, and as he walked the haunting fields of grain, he would have been desperate to resurrect his father's spirit in the wind-blown chaff that had supported them but which yielded little now but jarring visions. In bitter resignation Safa reasoned that he'd never really liked farming anyway and even if he did, there was something abhorrent about this land now. The rural hills of his countryside lost a treasure chest of memories with the brutal death of his father. While the Akchurins had had roots in this part of the world for hundreds of years—even as far back as the 15th century when Akchurin princes ruled Mordovia—it was under these circumstances that my grandfather became an emigrant, leaving his village never to return. And to further distance himself from Russia, my grandfather—although fully Mishar Tatar—adopted "Turkish" as his nationality, a decision that proved pragmatic while immigrating to the United States during the Cold War.

Although my grandfather shed the lifestyle of the countryside, he kept the acquired business and social talents of his father, and soon found a place for himself in the world of trade. He joined scores of refugees heading east in an exodus to Harbin, China—a city burgeoning with immigrants at the turn of the century. He soon began working in a clothing store, living in the bachelor's quarters provided by the store. While he was now 5,000 miles from home, Safa still enjoyed the company of his fellow Tatars, many of whom had also fled Ust Rakhmanovka and now lived in Harbin. One such Tatar neighbor was the young Maksura Fatima Altishe. Maksura was assimilating to Harbin quite well and soon caught the eye of the young Safa Akchurin.

Maksura was my grandmother, known to us grandchildren as *Aba*. As a child, I remember Aba as being very shy but that was mostly because of the language barrier. She was not fluent in English nor was I in Tatarça. It certainly did not keep her from recounting endless stories to my mother in her native tongue when she visited us. Often, my mother stood peeling potatoes as Aba sat telling her stories. "You know you have a very rich heritage," my mother would often tell me as I sat eating and listening to them. Aba was older then, very humble and grandmotherly. Needless to say I was surprised to later learn of her life as a youth.

Like Safa, Maksura was born in the country village of Ust Rakhmanovka. It was said that Maksura's father didn't care much for the countryside and preferred the city life. Consequently, he found employment as a *maître d'* in a nearby city, "commuting" back and forth. As the story goes, Maksura's mother began to suspect her husband was unfaithful and one day ventured to the city, unannounced, to see if her suspicions were true. They were. Her mother returned home. Eventually, Maksura's father came home as well—when he was older, dying of cancer. When the 1918 exodus to Harbin was underway, Maksura's mother was ready for another trip out of town, this time for good.

Maksura, like her father, took to city life. In Harbin she became an actress, the "prima donna" of the theater, as my uncle used to tease her.

"You don't understand. I was the belle of Harbin," she used to tell him.

My aunt Farida later concurred. "She really was famous in Harbin especially among the Russian community at the time. They would notice her in advertisements and come to see her."

Consequently, Maksura was said to have had quite a number of suitors in Harbin. Mindful of her father's past, Maksura's aunt took her aside and cautioned her to settle down and find herself a Tatar man. Safa and Maksura grew up in Ust Rakhmanovka but, ironically, they never met socially until Harbin. Maksura ultimately took her aunt's advice and began dating Safa. The two eventually married in Harbin and in 1920 Maksura gave birth to their first daughter, Farida. While the couple did not stay long in Harbin, others from their community did. Consequently, Harbin would be a city that held close ties for the couple for a long time.

By all accounts, my grandparents left Harbin simply in search of "a better life." They soon set their sights on Japan and the family moved to Kumamoto. There they had two more children, my mother Effat and my uncle Rashid. Several years later Safa and Maksura made a final move to the port city of Kobe where they gave birth to their second son, Shamil—my "Uncle Sam." Safa was soon self-employed in the import-export trade with his own shop in downtown Kobe. Maksura continued acting. She worked mostly in Kobe community plays that were open to the public. Often the plays were put on at the Mosque, downtown.

For two Mishar Tatars from a village of war-torn Russia, it had been a long journey for my grandparents Safa and Maksura, who now made their home in Japan. But Kobe would soon become an even more ominous stage with the approaching 1940s. War had a history of determining fate and would, like a hurricane, catapult the family's destiny once again while my mother would discover a most unexpected surprise—in the heart of war.

Circa 1919. My grandfather Safa Akchurin (far left) dons a taste for clothing in China while my grandmother Maksura (right), in full glory, seems to live up to her title as "the Belle of Harbin."

Harbin, China. Maksura holds center stage as she begins an acting career in Harbin—a passion she would continue to pursue even while raising a family later in cosmopolitan Kobe, Japan.

PART I: ANCESTRY • 21

The Republic of Mordovia sits just north of Penza, and 200 miles southeast of Moscow. My grandparents' birthplace of Ust Rakhmanovka is located between the capital of Saransk and the city of Krasnoslobodsk.

1894. A registration form confirms Safa's place of birth as May 10, 1894 in the village of Ust Rakhmanovka.

September 7, 1919. Safa and Maksura married in Harbin during the time of the Russian civil war. He was 25 and she was 17. My grandparents were married for 46 years until Safa passed away in 1965.

Ed's Family Tree: New England Bacons

At the other end of the world, my other grandfather prepares to leave the established countryside of his family as well—in western New York State.

At the turn of the 20th century, my grandfather, Harry Edward Bacon, was attending boarding school in New York's western Allegany County. Son of a hard-working entrepreneur and farmer, Harry grew up, like Safa, in the throes of rural upper income. It was not entirely clear, however, just how much Harry enjoyed it.

While Harry possessed a keen intellect, he also enjoyed the romp and raucousness of, shall we say, the more jovial crowds. His restless spirit often tagged those outside and on the fringe of the boarding school for late-night poker games, cigarette smoking, and the taste of Friday night liquor—the aroma of which was not lost on his most proper Aunt Aurelia, who happened to run the boarding school Harry was attending and more than once greeted him late at night. It wasn't long before Aurelia's face grew red from Harry's behavior and what she considered "keeping company with the wrong crowd." When Aurelia's verbal tirades ran their course, and apparently to no avail, she entered Harry's room one night at the witching hour and proceeded to purge Harry's belongings out the window. Then she dutifully locked up the house.

When Harry finally did arrive that night (or rather, early morning), the boarding house's unforgiving doorknob sent him into a state. He stealthily found a second window to plow through, claimed his remaining possessions, and never returned to Aunt Aurelia's quiet home. While my grandfather went on to become a surgeon, he retained that spicy spirit that made its debut in the halls of boarding school.

1885. Bacon & Peckham Grist Mill of Angelica is the large barn structure at left. Behind and right is a train station with a sitting train between the barn and depot. Photo courtesy of Robert Dorsey.

My grandfather was born in 1881 in Allegany County's Belmont, New York. His father Edward served in the Civil War and later made his fortune in business and farming—which included a grist mill, a meat market, and a 73-acre farm—as well as marrying into the then wealthy Hooker family of Allegany County, taking Mariah-Jean as his wife in 1872.

Harry, however, honed his interests towards college football, fishing, and medicine. According to newspaper accounts, after finishing high school, Harry entered Cornell University at Ithaca and completed a medical course at the Jefferson Medical College. He later took up an internship at the Johns Hopkins University in Baltimore, Maryland, where he also played on the Baltimore Medical College football team as a right tackle.[5]

Harry was soon ready to venture forth. His first move was to Denver, Colorado, to complete his medical training. In 1908, Denver and Gross College of Medicine of the University of Denver awarded the 27-year-old a Doctor of Medicine degree, a Surgeon's Certificate, and a license to practice medicine in the state of Colorado.

Harry located his first practice in Hugo, Colorado, where he also soon met and fell in love with a school teacher, one Lucylle Ann Hull, said to have been fresh off the train from the rolling hills of Nebraska. Lucylle, like Harry's mother Mariah, came from a large and well-educated family with diverse Christian persuasions. Both Harry and Lucylle had grown up on farms and both had lost a parent early in life. Harry's mother Mariah died at 44 of typhoid fever and Lucylle's father, Hiram Hull, was killed by lightning.

Harry and Lucylle grew inseparable. They married December 14, 1910, settled in Hugo, espoused the Episcopalian faith, and started a family, giving birth to Constance, Marjorie, and my father, Edward.

My grandfather's medical career was illustrious: sometimes tragic, sometimes humorous, and always driven by determination. Early in his career, Harry was called to a fire where a woman lay helpless with a 2 x 4 straight through her chest. Harry could only give her last rites. When my father was older, Harry believed he should expose his son to the realities of life. Harry would drag my father into the operating room and tell him to stand there and watch the surgery. Unfortunately, my father hated the smell of ether and spent most of the time vomiting. For all his good intentions, Harry found himself spending more time scolding and coaxing rather than teaching my father while, at the same time, ardently trying to complete the surgery. Still, Harry never gave up on the art of persuasion,

---

[5]December 16, 1943, *The Plainsman*. Hugo, Colorado.

however unconventional. My father often recalled the story of Dr. Bacon's approach to one patient's struggle with whiskey. The prescription: one (sugar) pill—with a strict warning that once the pill was taken the patient could never drink again as the combination would be lethal.

Circa 1915. (Left) Dr. Bacon at the wheel struts his 1910 Buick Runabout in Hugo (with unknown passengers). The vehicle served him well as households on the prairie kept him constantly moving.

After working the Midwest prairies for twenty years, Harry paused to consider. Then, in the late 1920s, he took a significant gamble and moved his entire family to the West Coast where he set up practice on San Francisco's Sutter Street.

By the time Harry had moved his family to San Francisco, my father was in high school and soon won a scholarship to the prestigious Montezuma Mountain School for Boys in Los Gatos, 35 miles south of San Francisco. Apparently, it was tough for my father to be separated from his family for the first time. Between September and December of that year, Harry wrote Ed six times, beginning each letter with *"My dear Ed,"*

> *... Now do not get homesick. You must remember how Connie was when she went to Berkeley—and had to do everything she did not want to do. Just remember all big successes have*

> *been hampered by adversities. Do each thing you are required to each day and top it off with a smile. If you have a few disappointments, remember your successes will be that much sweeter ....*

For the most part these were chatty letters, with lots of talk about football. Harry kept his growing health conditions from Ed, only mentioning "some lumbago" in a November letter. But Harry's personal medical diary was becoming quite another story, ending with a macabre sense of humor.

> *... In 1931 seized with violent abdominal pain most severe over both kidneys. Taken to SF hospital. X-rays showed pathological gall bladder with probable stones. Operation advised but refused due to relatives arriving from back East by which time condition improved. Next attack November 1931 followed by one every six months. January 1933 pain in both legs and feet. Went to St. Helena Sanatorium for two weeks, felt better. October 1933 developing oedema in left leg and all muscles to the neck are sore to the touch. Lately, short of breath with slight distress in region of the heart.*
>
> *Habits: Terrible. Three packs of cigarettes daily, considerable sherry, wine, and beer. Irregular eating habits. Underscore recommendations: Firing squad, guillotine, noose, lethal gas.*

On December 11, 1934, Harry ends his last letter by telling Ed how much he is looking forward to seeing him at Christmas and how proud he is of him. Sadly, Harry would not get to see Christmas nor his son. Five days later, Dr. Harry Edward Bacon lay dead on an operating table in San Francisco's Mt Zion Hospital due to complications from removing his gallstones. At the age of 19, my father had shared the family fate of losing a parent young in life.

The Bacons shared many things with the Akchurins although, geographically, they were worlds apart. Both my great-grandfathers became successful entrepreneurs, faced the trauma of civil war in their respective countries, and, ultimately, had sons—my grandfathers—who were risk-takers, educated, and adventurous, leaving their respective homelands, traveling thousands of miles in order to start new lives. They were in different worlds yet many of their family values were mirror images. Maybe it is not so strange that my parents would ultimately pair up. If they were lucky, their shared values would attract each other while their differences would perhaps complement an otherwise unlikely meeting. As the 1930s progressed, now all that separated the two families was the Pacific Ocean and the destiny of the 1940s.

1910. Lucylle and Harry Bacon. The doctor at his office (below).

30 • ED & IVET

Circa 1880. My great grandparents (upper left) Edward and Mariah Bacon post Civil War. A much older Edward (upper right, circa 1895) remained a widower after Mariah's death. (Lower, clockwise): Harry, Edward, Harry's sisters Mabelle, Pearl and Eleanor shown at their home in Allegany County's Angelica, New York. Photos courtesy of Joy Martin and Robert Dorsey.

PART TWO: MY PARENTS' EARLY YEARS

Ed's Early Years: "Edd"

While the Akchurins settle in Kobe, the Bacons move several times during my father's early years, finally making San Francisco their home. Then, in his early 20s, Ed follows his father's footsteps by taking his own journey far from home.

~~~~~~

The kindness of youth is in its resilience and the ability to adapt. Even when love is distant, children will search it out and find it somewhere. And loneliness does not always result in sadness although it can affect direction later in life. My father was a good example of this. As a lonely child, he often found love from the dependable smoothness of his collie's coat, in the anxious approaches of his pet pigeons and doves, and from the loyal ecstasy of chocolates, pies, and cakes. He was a lonely boy but he was not unhappy.

My father was born on July 27, 1915 in Hugo, Colorado. His father omitted the name "Harry" on the birth certificate, instead listing

H. Edward Bacon Jr. as my father's "full" name. His two older sisters enjoyed calling him *Junior* and sometimes *Curly* (for his blond hair), both names he disliked. He preferred the name *Edd*—as he spelled it in his younger years.

Most significant in my father's early profile is the portrait of a loner captured poignantly in a boating story. When he was 7, his mother took him for a drive miles away to a lake where there was a small row boat. She dropped him off—alone—and picked him up hours later. One pictures a curly blond-haired kid out in the middle of a lake, thinking of ways to entertain himself.

"Things were different back then," he recalled. "Nowadays, my god, I would never think of dropping my kid off in the middle of nowhere like that. That boat could have had a hole in it for all we knew," he laughed.

This lifestyle was not unique to my father. My great-grandfather Edward had sisters but no brothers. My grandfather Harry had sisters but no brothers. Likewise, my father had sisters but no brothers and his father was a busy physician who moved the family frequently. I used to wonder why my father never had any friends when I was growing up. Now I think perhaps it wasn't so much a choice. Like father like son. This lonely profile was now three generations old and led my dad to be not antisocial but asocial. If you grow up on the moon, you may not necessarily dislike people but there's not going to be anyone there to engage with and your social skills will suffer, however wonderful you may be.

Whether it was being an only son, having an on-call physician for a father, growing up in the relatively sparse plains of the Midwest, or a combination of all of the above—my father's personality was shaped, in part, by coping with a lonely childhood in a growing state of self-reliance. What saved him was that his family, although preoccupied, loved him dearly. He often recalled how he was once scolded at the dinner table and sent to his room only later to discover his grandmother standing outside his room pretending to further yell at him, then stepping inside and placing a piece of chocolate cake next to his bed. Later, when he was away at school, his father took time out to send him weekly personal letters and his mother, while as prim and proper as they come, fully validated my father by later forever welcoming my mother to her home and her family.

When Edd was 5, the Bacons moved north of Hugo to Fort Collins. As a child, he adapted to his sparse social landscape by discovering animals and sweets to be irresistible friends. In Fort Collins, his beloved collie Cicero learned to know just when school was out and would go down the street to meet Edd. Together they would first head home to see how Edd's birds were doing. According to his sister Marge, Edd had amassed quite a collection of pigeons and doves that he learned to raise. In Fort Collins, his father invested in a bakery, which was next on the list. Between Cicero, his flock of birds, and the family bakery, Edd learned to fill an otherwise lonesome after-school schedule.

Later as an adult, my father maintained his hobby with aviaries, he was never without the companionship of a family dog, and a chocolate shake remained his favorite afternoon treat.

In 1929 the family made a final move to San Francisco. Three months later the stock market crashed. Edd was fortunate. As the son of a physician, he was spared the devastation many Americans endured at the time. Trouble would track him down later.

While my mother would emerge as the picture of poise, charm, and domesticity during the 1930s, my father reflected a more impetuous personality during his high school years. This is a time I picture him in corduroy trousers and a block sweater by day and Ricky Racer leather by night. He shared that upscale yet defiant spirit that his father possessed and was also drawn to the "fast" crowd from which he would reap the rewards and consequences. By high school he was still a loner but now restless.

Edd first attended Lowell High School in San Francisco where he met school buddies Ginney Dowd, Zane Stickel, and his best friend Bill Bowman—all avid football players. His interests soon turned to cars and motorcycles, according to his sister Marge. "One day he and Bill Bowman decided to take their bikes out zooming up and down the hills of San Francisco. So intent were they on the fun they were having that they didn't notice when they sped right past Dad driving his car. There was quite a storm in our house that night."

"Stormy" was exactly how Harry would define his son's growing temperament. Like a new set of wings sprouting, Edd was discovering an energy the football field was apparently not sufficient to handle. Those wheels to his motor bike found ways to sneak out and continue their quest until they finally hit a brick wall in the form of a San Francisco police officer who, not surprisingly, became intent on putting a cap on this speed demon. In the course of issuing Edd a citation, words ensued and, as the story goes, the officer called Edd a "son of a bitch" to which my father responded by decking the cop. Marge recalled, "When Dad went to get Edd out of jail, things were smoothed over because Edd explained that the name calling was a reflection on his mother." With tongue in cheek Marge later quipped, "He probably got another piece of cake too."

1918. Edd, Marge, and Connie (top left) pose in front of Lucylle's touring car. Harry, the kids, and Cicero (top right) show off a day's catch at Colorado's West Lake outside Denver. Edd in a variety of uniforms: (bottom, left to right) a 1917 stars and stripes suit at his first home in Hugo; a 1920s school uniform in an ardent pose with Cicero and Harry at Poudre River; and in a 1930s Montezuma football jersey crouched and ready for play.

Actually, Marge wasn't too far off. Harry, ever the pragmatist, later tapped into Edd's self-reliance in an effort to tame this bottle rocket. As a physician, Harry was treating more and more auto accident victims and grew to hate the idea of his son racing around town. So Harry made a deal with Edd and purchased a Ford Model T, agreeing that Edd could have the car if he disassembled it and put it back together—by himself. The challenge suited Edd. Ultimately, he accepted the task and won the Ford.

This was also the time Edd hooked up with high-school sweetheart Arlene Chamberlain, a relationship that seemed to be as topsy-turvy as the streets of San Francisco. The couple broke up and got together more times than Edd could count. Not surprisingly, at this time, Harry also moved tactfully to redirect his son's moral compass by encouraging Edd to apply for a scholarship to the polished and regimented Montezuma School for Boys, a change of venue—in the enticing Santa Cruz Mountains. Harry's efforts proved successful. Edd eventually got the scholarship as well.

In 1935 Edd graduated from Montezuma. It was a bitter sweet time. He was thrilled to graduate while poised for another scholarship. But as the celebration wore off, the reality of his father's untimely death resurfaced. Graduation seemed a hollow victory without his dad to celebrate with. For the first time, Edd was despondent. He felt aimless as summer approached. His mother (who had found direction herself on a journey from home as a youngster) encouraged him to get out and take a trip around the United States with Bill Bowman.

Heading out with a long list of relatives to visit, Edd and his friend took off in the summer of '35. The two left with a mere $25 a piece, working as they traveled. Edd learned to pilot a Cessna and to master circus fire-eating; he saw the country and caught up with relatives. The summer proved a good elixir.

Tragically, Edd would later lose this best friend as well. After the war, Bill became a policeman in San Francisco. While heading out on an emergency call one night, his motorcycle skidded and crashed on the oil-soaked pavement. Bill died the next day. This story always broke my heart knowing how few close friends my father had and, consequently, how honored I felt when I first learned that my father had named me after his best friend.

1930s-40s. Edd's sister Marge (upper left, 1944) recalled the days when Edd (upper right, 1932) was clocked at 96 mph by the police while out enjoying high-performance driving through the hills of San Francisco. An older and wiser Edd (lower right, 1935) just before the cross-country drive that he took with friend Bill Bowman (lower left).

Back home after his cross-country trip with Bill, Edd found that the football scholarship had arrived in the mail. It was from Santa Clara University, a local Jesuit school. But Edd was not ready to return to studies or football. Studies were too passive for his restless soul. And football, while aggressive and fun, was recreational. What Edd wanted was a job—something that would keep his restless attention with a substantial reward. Although just 20, with his father gone, Edd was feeling the approach of adulthood, even shedding his youthful signature "Edd" for the more grown-up "Ed."

An enormous construction project was underway in San Francisco at the time: *the Golden Gate Bridge*. Ed began working on the bridge in the fall of 1936 as an employee of Maaco Construction as a mechanic apprentice. Dad recalled that employees were not allowed to smoke on the job, so he would simply walk a little higher up the cable expanse. There in the infamous San Francisco fog, he would be undetected savoring his Lucky Strikes.

By the end of the year, Ed quit his job on the bridge in order to go to work for T.E. Connoly, who was carving out the adjoining Golden Gate Tunnel in Sausalito. It was a very cold dripping tunnel, especially when one worked the night shift. Ed recalled how he would gaze over to see the city lights and imagine all those people nice and warm in their homes.

Not long after, Ed seemed to have gotten construction out of his system and found himself drawn again to academics. He enrolled in San Francisco's Lincoln University of Law, while working for the Federal Housing Administration as an appraiser.

About this time, nasty things were beginning to brew around the world. By 1939 Franco had become dictator in Spain, Stalin had taken a strong hold in Russia, and Germany had begun invading Europe. World War II was brewing. And while it seemed far away at the moment, the war was getting ready to reach out and wrap its long ugly tendrils around Ed.

Ultimately, Ed had gotten back together with Arlene. After high school, they broke up at least three times and re-married twice. It was, at best, a roller-coaster ride. While my father's sense of self-reliance was showing no signs of weakness, his social skills were still underdeveloped.

By the time Ed was in law school, the couple had been re-married a year. Sadly, Ed's roller coaster soon jumped the rails completely. With college studies and work, Ed normally ate lunch out. One day he decided to stop in and have lunch at home, only to find dear Arlene sandwiched between the sheets with another man. Not surprisingly, Dad called it quits with Arlene. By June of that year, the couple was granted an Interlocutory Divorce—essentially a legal separation.

Also not surprising, that year Ed decided to leave school, leave his job, and even leave the country. Bacons are good at restless. Ed found his brother-in-law's advice irresistible: sign up with J. H. Pomeroy, a large construction firm, in Guam. Ed could get his mind off things, go have another adventure, and this time make some good money. Whether it was the loss of his father or the discovery of a cheating wife, as an adult Ed's remedy was to retreat inward, take to the road, and then turn to physical work to cope with the heartaches of life.

My father's early years left him with strengths and challenges. Close friends were few and far between. To compensate for this gap, my father tapped into creativity, adventure, and industrious employment much like his father and grandfather before him. Like his forefathers as well, talkative and extroverted women in particular were very appealing, filling the equation that opposites attract. If he was lucky, those women would also have character and credibility. But my father was finding himself not as lucky with his Arlene. Of course, "it takes two to tango," and while my father was good-looking, football-league material, and well employed, he was often more pensive than talkative, which can sometimes work against a relationship.

Self-reliant people, like my father, do well to remember to come "out" of themselves when the world wants to engage them. For my dad, this was his stuck valve, his rusty door that failed to operate freely, allowing the impression that he was distant, or worse, indifferent. In fact, his lawyer-like mind was quite engaged in human drama, his Leo-heart was perpetually generous, and his dry sense of humor touched everyone he knew—when he *did* come to the table. Self-reliance has its limits. One can find comfort and security in years of emotional fortressing, which can itself be a formidable competitor to love.

It was my father's challenge to remember that life does not forever lead you to a lonely lake or unrequited love or snatch best friends from you, and that while self-reliance is a worthy survival instinct, he had to learn to share himself by also being vulnerable through trust and hope in order to reap the best life has to offer. He had not quite learned to do that yet. That was something my mother was poised to teach him.

It was in this emotional context that Ed stood on a San Francisco dock on a bright summer afternoon in 1941, with his mother, sisters, and friends, who joined him in a farewell as he boarded the *USS Matsoni* headed for

Guam. At least one familiar face was joining Ed on the adventure as well: his old school buddy Zane Stickel.

"It was a beautiful day. My mother and my friends were there. I had my luggage, my typewriter, and my liquor and I was ready to go," Ed recalled. It was only five months before the attack on Pearl Harbor and, unawares, Ed was heading straight into the South Pacific. It would prove to be the ultimate test of his self-reliance and vulnerability as well as the ideal time for my mother to enter the picture.

Ivet's Early Years: "Effie"

Every drama seems to have a calm before the storm. In this story, no one better represents that than my mother, Ivet. Her childhood memories are a contrast to what she would face as a young adult.

If ever there was a person who had whimsical contradictions, it was my mother. Painfully shy yet loved having her picture taken. Glamorous but without egocentricity. Socially inclined yet without the gift of gab. Highly respectful of authority while harboring a polished streak of independence. She even loved to gamble—but always gave her winnings away!

One thing that was never contradictory was her care and love for people, the result of a family's ancestral tradition of hospitality. It was said that my great-grandfather Çerulla's village farm was a place where a traveler could stop, rest, and feed his horse—even trade a horse for a younger one. My mother had one of those families where the weary instantly felt welcomed and cared for. Hospitality was a highly regarded priority based in her family's religious tradition, all of which was second nature to my mother. Her family and their Tatar community had a fabric about them as tight, embroidered, and ancestral as a cherished Persian rug. The social dynamics and support that my mother was able to take for granted was a kind of wealth unfamiliar to my father. It was almost tangible, accented by warm, welcoming smiles, the soothing aroma of home cooking, the immediate attention to helping a visitor with his coat, or the touch of a guiding arm to a seat, the unasked-for cup of tea, even the ubiquitous doilies that adorned the house that said we have prepared for you, the visitor, and your creature comforts. It came to be as though every gesture my mother made was born of this inherited culture of nurture and service to others.

But none of this can be fully appreciated without understanding that the entire culture my mother's family lived and breathed was accentuated by the enchanting sounds of their native tongue, a Finno-Ugric dialect of Tatarça. My mother spoke an exotic, guttural language that gave her and her relatives noticeable accents whenever they spoke English.

"Khi Beal, khow arrr yeuw?" one relative might ask me.

To me that sound was intoxicating. Although I was raised in the United States, our living room could fill to the brim in no time with the rapture of those foreign-sounding voices. Add to that a sea of red lipstick, coiffed hairdos, cocktail dresses, suits, ties, cologne, cordiality, and warm humor and, as a youngster, I found myself nearly delirious in this unusual family setting, all of which echoed a culture somewhere very far away.

My mother, Ivet Akchurin Bacon, was born on July 7, 1924, in Kumamoto, Japan, with a first name that took on quite an evolution itself. Her Turkish given name was *Effat*, a Mishar version of the Arabic *Iffat* meaning *virtuous*. Throughout her childhood, she was affectionately known as *Effie*. Even her grade-school report cards use this name. When I was growing up, my cousins called her *Effatapah*, the ending signifying *Aunt*. Later, as a young adult, she would morph the Arabic *Iffat* with the French *Yvette* spelling it simply, *Ivet*.

By 1941, my mother's family was living in the hills of Kobe, above the port city in the Aotami neighborhood, at No. 45 Kagoike Dori 3 Chome. Interestingly, their home sat in the hills of Kobe much like how our home in the Burlingame hills nestled itself above San Francisco Bay.

With a father in the field of trade and a mother no stranger to the stage, one might expect my mother to have been an extremely extroverted person. While her brother Shamil was, my mother was—contradictorily—far more subdued. Homemaking was her passion. She often showed her mother photos of homes with extravagant perennial gardens, insisting *that* would be where she would live someday. When asked of her childhood, not surprisingly, what she first recalled was the inside of her home. While their first home in Kumamoto had been Japanese in style, their home in Kobe was a two-story, four-bedroom European number. It was wall-shingled and painted rustic red with white trim and had a balcony overlooking the Kobe harbors.

Kobe Mosque. Effie, upper right. Shamil sitting, lower center.

"The home had a large entrance hall. To the left, the maid's quarters. To the right, a big kitchen. The living room and the dining room were divided by sliding doors. In the entrance hall was a spiral staircase. The first door at the top of the stairs was my room. Next to me my brothers shared a room. My sister and my parents also had their own rooms."

Ivet's social surroundings were also cozy. It had been a good 25 years since Maksura and Safa had emigrated from Ust Rakhmanovka. By now the family had an enormous network of friends and relatives in Kobe, most of whom had ties to their religious community as well. Aunts and uncles lived in the same neighborhood. Ivet's cousin Aisha lived next door. Their community center and mosque were a few miles away, as were other social venues such as the Kobe Regatta & Athletic Club (the KRAC) and the Shioya Club. This type of social support was an advantage Ivet would continue to enjoy throughout her life.

Whenever Ed's father moved his family, they had moved alone. But whenever Maksura and Safa moved, they did so with fellow Tatars. However distant the move, there was always a familiar face at the destination. Nor was it uncommon for a family to add on a bedroom to their home to accommodate a newly married daughter and her husband. Aspects of this tight-knit structure were something my mother later struggled with losing after moving to the United States. When my oldest sister graduated from high school and wanted to find an apartment with her girlfriends, my mother was absolutely baffled. She had no point of reference for such an arrangement. It took a long time for her to understand what she perceived as a detached American teenage custom. It was even worse when I moved out—which was not down the street but to another state. The day after I proposed moving, my mother was taken to the hospital for what was described as "a mild heart attack." In my mother's world, if someone left the house, it was to marry. Why else on earth would you leave?

Very different from my father's upbringing was also *where* my mother grew up. Not just another country but in the hustle and bustle of a major metropolitan city as opposed to the quiet countryside. While Ivet, that is *Effie*, began kindergarten in Kumamoto, she grew up in Kobe beginning in her grade-school years. Next to the imposing Kobe Mosque was a Turkish school that taught first through sixth grade. After finishing there, the Tatar children would either go to the neighboring Catholic school or the Canadian Academy. Safa chose to send his sons to the Canadian Academy and his daughters to the Catholic Ecole Sainte Marie. My uncle Rashid recalled the ethnic diversity of the schools in Kobe.

"Looking back now I wonder how any of us students understood each other. There were so many different nationalities: Germans, Italians, Chinese, Jewish. Everyone had their own unusual dialect and yet, somehow, we found a way to communicate with each other."

My mother remembered the cosmopolitan nature of Kobe during her school years as well as its sometimes dizzying effect on her. "We used to have French class in the morning and English in the afternoon. Then, I would talk with my Japanese friends at lunch and later speak Tatarça at dinner at home. Sometimes my head would be spinning with so many languages going through my mind."

Kobe 1931. (Top) My grandmother's Arabic handwriting reads: *Students of Islamic school in Kobe with their Teacher. Graduation memory. June 21, 1931. Kobe.* Before attending Kobe's Ecole St Marie, Effie attended a Tatar pre-school. The bright summer sun captures (bottom L-R) sister Farida standing in front of the teacher, Effie who stands front and left of Farida, and younger brother Rashid second from the right in the front row.

Again, it was home where my mother excelled, and one thing she easily learned to master was Far Eastern cooking. She was an attentive student of her mother and aunts, who taught her Turkish, Russian, Indian, Chinese, and Japanese dishes. My favorite was her currie-and-rice decked with chopped pickles, bananas, hard-boiled eggs, and raisins. The most popular dish was her *peremeches* (fried beef patties wrapped in pleated dough). People would cancel plans if they learned Mom was making peremeches on Sunday. She also treated us to sukiyaki, chicken-and-rice pilaf, beef stroganoff, *pelmenis* (Russian dumplings), Japanese pickled radish with rice, apricot pastries, and honey-doused çäk-çäk (pronounced "check-check"), a holiday dessert and also considered the official Tatar wedding cake. And those were just a few of the Eastern gems she would toss in for a change of pace. There is something about a mother's cooking that is not only able to transform food but love into substance, texture, smells, and tastes in a way that bears the unique memories of that one who loved and cared for you. My Aunt Farida said that often Baba would be found crying just from the sheer memory of his mother's cooking—a trait I have shared more than once with my grandfather.

My mother was just 17 the summer my father left for Guam. It was a time of stark contrast to the years that would follow as my mother recalled. "I remember those as very happy and carefree days in my life. Mother gave me a beautiful birthday party at the Club. We had music and we danced until midnight. My first formal dance party. I had a yellow organdy dress with tiny white flowers and Mother had given me a string of pearls. I think it was one of my happiest birthdays."

Summer was Effie's favorite time of year. She often spent day after day on Suma Beach. I used to call my mother "Olive Oyl" after the Popeye cartoon character. In her youth, photos captured her tall gait with her long skinny legs, or showed her sunbathing or posing in her swim suit. Perhaps if you grow up in Japan, you are, by nature, part fish. I don't recall anyone who loved the water more than my mother's family. Half their photos were beach shots. They even learned how to float in a unique way in which both their head and toes remained above water. As kids we used to call it the "mommy thing" as we sank to our chins, laughing and desperately trying to mimic them.

In addition to the sea, Effie enjoyed climbing the hills of nearby Mt. Rokko with her friends. "They had a beautiful teahouse on Mt. Rokko with a ledger book to sign in. I'll bet it's still there with my name in it."

Kobe, Japan circa 1935. My mother's family, left to right: my mother "Effie," Maksura, Farida, Safa, Rashid and, center front, Shamil. The family lived in the hills of the Aotami neighborhood in a red European-style house.

But her favorite summer activities were the Kobe port festivals and chief among them was the large 4th of July fair. "I used to come home with all sorts of prizes. Everything was free—ice cream, popcorn, cotton candy, and sandwiches. I remember picking up little American flags there."

Effie would be forced to grow up very quickly in the years following, and one of those little American flags that she picked up at the port festival would find itself adorning a most unusual vehicle, one that would further escort Effie into adulthood.

My mother's early memories are indicative of her personality. Generally, she had an optimistic aura about her. The crescent moon is a symbol of Islam just as it is of my mother. She was a child of the moon—dreamy, sultry, moody, yet keenly aware. The biblical call to be "as wise as serpents and gentle as doves" aptly described her personality. She was spiritual and extremely intuitive.

The first time I tried smoking cigarettes, my mother's "sixth sense" left an indelible memory on me. I was 13 and had gone with my school friends to downtown Burlingame. We all snuck away to a nearby creek and lit up. Later, I hitchhiked home all the while quite nauseous. When I got home, I went straight to the upstairs bathroom and vomited. Much later that evening at dinner, my mother said, "So you started smoking, huh?" I think I coughed up my soup. I remember thinking how on earth did she pick that up? It had been hours ago and miles away. I realized that day there were absolutely no limits to her radar.

Reason, logic, and dogma are driving forces for many parents. However, what my mother brought to the world was nurture, belief, compassion, service, art, devotion, domesticity, love—and intuition. She was not trained in horticulture, but I used to tell people that my mother could make plants bloom by looking at them. She was an artist—not only stocking her gardens to the hilt but curving her plant beds, arranging floral vases, sketching charcoal drawings; even her housekeeping had a refined art about it as she single-handedly maintained an immaculate home that, nevertheless, was occupied by five manic children and two adults.

Circa 1947. (Left) Safa, facing north, stands outside the family's Kobe home. (Right) Maksura, facing south, stands with Farida's children Rawilla and Shamil across the street from the family's shingled home to the right.

Nurturing sometimes took my mother over the top. So strong was her love of anything living she found it hard to have pets, the most innocent forms of life. I was always puzzled why she never wanted our dog in the house. Then, when I was ten, my dog was hit by a car in front of our home. My mother was inconsolable. "This is why I can't have animals," she said as she walked away crying. Like the sense of taste, nurturing was a "sense" to my mother—but a heightened one. Just as a high-pitched sound can torture someone with keen hearing, her sense of compassion could, at times, overwhelm her. It was not that she abhorred pets; rather, it was that she instinctively knew the cost of that care when they were lost or injured. Already overwhelmed with a heightened concern for people, she instinctively sensed that adding pets to her affections would simply be too much.

She was often perceived as starry-eyed. But while she believed in God, fate, and the moon and the stars, her highly evolved intuition protected her optimistic spirit from being taken advantage of. She could spot a fake a mile away and was not hesitant to let slip the occasional not-so-subtle perception of a prospective friend you might bring home.

I don't remember many bedtime stories but do remember her feeding us, clothing us, driving us, holding us, always being home for us. She was short on sermons and long on actions.

Perhaps most significant is that Effie grew up to be a wonderful balance to Ed who, with his Scotch-Irish-English descent, was less emotional and more practical, logical, and comical, making him perfectly suited for a dreamy and embracing crescent moon-child from the East.

Circa 1940. (top) Ivet poses at her favorite Suma Beach. (bottom) She stands tallest (in white swim suit) alongside school friends enjoying the summer sun and one of her favorite sports: swimming.

PART THREE: ED'S CAPTURE

1941: Ed Ventures to Guam

Ed's Homeric journey to the South Pacific eventually brings him to a tropical paradise. At least it appears that way at first.

It is eerie to recall now that as my father boarded the *USS Matsoni*, his ship was heading to Honolulu, and its first stop was, of all places, Pearl Harbor. He was there only a few days in order to change ships, clueless that in five months the Japanese would ravage that very harbor.

In Honolulu Ed transferred off the *Matsoni* and boarded the *USS Bridge*, which is where he met Arthur "Woody" Woodruff. Woody had the classic tall-dark-and-handsome look, but he also had intelligence to match, often reading a book a day. Woody was in charge of a large number of men on the ship. Those, like my father, who were transferring from the *Matsoni* added significantly to the crew of the *Bridge*. Ed recalled being assigned to first class but he found it stuffy. He had much more fun at the lower deck card games where he'd head down with Zane Stickel and Woody.

When the vessel had crossed the 180th meridian, Ed began to see some very strange things.

"We saw U.S. naval ships practicing shooting. There was live ammunition fire. Also, there were black-outs on board at night. It seemed odd.

Maybe they knew something. We knew there was war in Germany but not out here. Certainly we had no idea there would be war with Japan."

The ship's first stop was to be Wake Island, but a typhoon took the ship off course. "For two days we had to tie equipment and lunch trays down. The Plan B was to go to Midway Island instead."

Plan B worked and so the first landing since Honolulu was Midway. Ed had never seen sand so white before. But even more entertaining were the Gooney birds, who were adept at landing on water but whose attempts on land were usually comic disasters. Ed was also amused at the bird's local notoriety in things such as the Gooneyville Gazette, Gooney Avenue, and the Gooney Tavern. After Midway, the *USS Bridge* decided to skip Wake Island entirely and head straight for Guam.

When Ed landed on Guam, he was immediately hit with some rather interesting news. Seems the contractors were offering huge incentives for workers to stay longer than previously agreed to. The incentives were in the form of enormous bonuses. Ed wrote home,

If I stay out the year and don't return to the U.S., I will get my salary plus half of it for every month I stay here.

It might have been a good time for him to recall those suspicions he had felt at the 180th meridian that "maybe they knew something." Instead, Ed settled in and took to the sights and sounds of his new home. But first he had to deal with a small matter in his own quarters as he noted in a letter home.

Last night I lost my mustache but it took three guys to do it. Stickel is just like Ginney in size and Tiny is one of the largest men here at 295 pounds. Stickel and Tiny said they would take me down and shave off my mustache and I told them it would take more than the two of them to do it. Well it's off but it took three of them to do it because my 6-foot-roommate helped them. Our room looks like it was hit by a typhoon.

Ed signed off his first letter quite optimistic at the prospects of making money, especially if he could manage to stay an extra five years. It would seem that the powers that be had Ed (and no doubt, quite a few others) right where they wanted him. At least Ed's optimism is an interesting contrast to a report later issued to the Secretary of the Navy by then Governor of Guam U.S. Navy Captain G. J. McMillian:

> The political situation in the Pacific was assumed tense during the summer of 1941. After an effort extending over several months, arrangements were finally made to evacuate all dependents, including civilians from Guam ....[6]

Just prior to arriving in Guam, Ed was told he was going to be assigned clerical work, as Paymaster. Ed strongly protested, telling them he didn't know a damn thing about being a paymaster. But he was told the current paymaster was quitting and that they would train Ed when he arrived. It was another story that revealed my father's impetuous side, which was at odds with his sisters' unconvincing concerns for protocol.

"By the time I arrived, the paymaster had already left. For the first three months, it was crazy because the former paymaster was behind in his paperwork. Then it came close to Thanksgiving and one of the supervisors came to me and said we'd have to postpone paying the men a week. I told them the hell with that. These guys are Union men and that's not going to fly. We got in a big quarrel and I knocked him clear off his feet, he went flying out of the trailer. So he went and told some other supervisor and threatened to have me fired.

"Soon I got a letter from Connie, who somehow found out about this brawl, telling me I was going to get fired and had disgraced the whole family and on and on and what the hell was I doing?

"Then Pomeroy himself showed up. He was a big fella. I took my letter from Connie and asked him if he'd explain this letter. Pomeroy looked at it and then asked, 'Who the hell is this Connie?' I told him she was my sister. He said, 'What the hell is a big guy like you working as a paymaster for anyway? You oughta be out in the field somewhere.' I told him that was fine with me. So he said he'd make me truck foreman and sent me off."

With overtime and bonuses as a truck foreman, Ed was now earning about $240 a month. Teacher salaries in the US at the time were about

---

[6] *Guam Recorder*. (1972). University of Guam, Micronesian Area Research Center, 2:(2-3)

$160 a month.[7] He was not completely oblivious to the notion now that war could break out. And his next letter home suggested that many men were growing unhappy with the situation and were starting to leave. Nevertheless, Ed had no intention of leaving. He was making good money and beginning to admire people like Pomeroy and Connie's husband Louis back home—men who started from the bottom and worked their way up. He was in his element. Ed was getting trained left and right. He was pumped up and appeared as tough as the Capras Island he was currently working on, as he described in a letter home.

It is a very weird island with no trees. The only things living on the island are lizards and iguanas. The rock is so hard and jagged that shoes only last about 3 weeks.

Unfortunately, the promising career on Guam would be cut short. Ed's last letter home from Guam could be a page taken straight out of *Paradise Lost*. The letter, dated December 2, 1941, was only one week before Ed would find himself fighting for his life.

I sure wish you folks could spend a week here. There are sights here that photographs could never capture. The ocean water is deep blue and crystal clear. You can see clear to the bottom to the colored coral. Hundreds of different colored fish and sea animals as well as different sea flowers I have never seen before.

When the moon shines through the coconut trees and reflects on the water, it makes such a tropical scene. And when the sun sets, you see double. As it sets in the west, you can see the reflection in the east as well.

The last two lines are prophetic. Ed saw the East and the West converging into a mirroring of one another. Yet he could never have known how the East and West would soon be drawn together in such a dramatic and personal way.

---

[7]kclibrary.lonestar.edu/decade40.html

PART III: ED'S CAPTURE • 59

Postage as exotic as his island maps out Ed's journey from San Francisco to the South Pacific paradise of Guam.

Japanese Attack: Ed Is Captured

E D'S PARADISE VANISHES IN AN INSTANT, AS JAPANESE FORCES INVADE GUAM, TURNING HIS DREAM INTO A NIGHTMARE.

※※❁※※

While the summer of 1941 was a pleasant one for Ed on his tropical island and for Ivet with her innocent summer vacation, it was a purely evil summer in other parts of the world. By this time, German Nazis were ordering Jews to wear the Star of David. They were also invading the Soviet Union and conducting mass murders at Kiev. And while Ivet described her days as "carefree," the political situation of Japan was anything but.

Japan's geopolitical situation had been very complex throughout the late 1930s. By 1941 the nation was engaged in conflict with China. Some argue Japan was securing her interests and those of the Far East in general. Others argue Japan was an aggressor.

The U.S. and other Western countries were among those who interpreted Japan's activities towards China as aggressive. The U.S. and others adopted embargoes against Japan. Japanese leaders countered that Japan was attempting to stabilize the region and that the embargoes were short-sighted and meddling, not to mention potentially disastrous to the

Japanese economy. The Japanese grew increasingly infuriated, culminating with a military campaign.[8]

One of Japan's planned targets was a harbor on the Hawaiian Islands. On December 7, 1941, while Ed was still on Guam and Ivet was back in school, the Japanese government altered the fate of millions with the notorious air attack on Pearl Harbor, ushering in a hurricane of events.

The island of Guam was slated to be next. Although Pearl Harbor had just been struck, by the next day there had been no news of it on Guam. Like Pearl Harbor, the subsequent attack on Guam took the Americans completely by surprise. My father's eyewitness account captures the pandemonium at his Sumay barracks in Guam on the early morning of December 8, 1941, and the days that followed. This was a story my father was asked to repeat often during those Sunday night dinners at our home in California. My shorthand course in high school paid off. I finally transcribed the story during one of those dinners as my father once again recalled the horror.

"At the end of my night shift, I passed by Petrovitch. He had just cooked up a ton of glazed donuts. They were the last good meal I had. I got to bed about 8 a.m. with only about a half-hour of sleep. Suddenly, I woke to the sounds of explosives and aircraft. Planes often stopped at Sumay for refueling. But all this sounded different.

"I jumped up and looked out to see that the entire lumber shop had been blown up. Next thing I knew the whole damn camp was blowing up all around me. I looked up again and saw a plane, then looked down and saw Stubbe, who was half-deaf. I ran down the hall yelling, 'COME ON, STUBBE, THE WAR IS ON!'

"We ran as fast as we could to the coral caves outside the camp and ducked inside for cover. I kept wondering, 'Where are the Americans?' And then I kept telling myself, 'They'll be here tomorrow.' We had three raids that morning.

"When the planes left, we went back to the camp. The head of the Marines had posted a notice: 'WAR IS ON.' We were to report to the

---

[8] *The Library of Congress World War II Companion*. (2007). NY: Simon and Schuster, 75-113.

Marines barracks. When we got there, we were issued guns half-full of ammo. No one knew what to do.

"Then we were given our first orders: to dynamite. We had some big trucks. Those Euclids had 6 gears just to go backwards. We were to round up those and our tractor shovels and blow them up to keep the Japanese from using them. We blew up everything. First we machine-gunned all the tires and engines of all rolling equipment and dynamited all the larger equipment, the shovels, draglines, and Cats. Harley Lucke was a 300-pound fella that I worked with. He and I were also issued 45's and ordered to help protect the island. We were to patrol the main street in Agat for the first two nights.

"On December 10th, the Japanese started landing. At that time Lucke and I were issued a truck and ordered to evacuate the native Chamorros from Agana. On our third trip, we were machine-gunned by Japanese who had, by then, taken over Agana. We lost three civilians but were able to get the rest of the group to the hills. I was then ordered to take the truck and destroy it. The Japanese were already in Agat when I sent the truck over an embankment.

"It quickly became pandemonium. Everybody ran for the hills. I later hooked up with Woody and Zane, and we took off for the boondocks where we set up a makeshift camp. What little water we could find we tried to boil, especially since we were only able to grab a few bottles of Tom Collins mix, which actually ends up making you thirstier when you drink it straight.

"We soon found we were dying of thirst. We got so thirsty we were drinking out of muddied water buffalo holes. We drank the water anyway and somehow it didn't affect us. The next thing I remember we came upon our houseboy, who was a Chamorro. He used to help us back at the barracks.

"'Everyone's gone back to the barracks. You guys are the only ones left, come on,' he said.

"We fell for it. We went to get picked up by what we thought were the Marines but instead were picked up by the Japanese. He'd turned us in. The Japanese were all carrying machine guns. They lined us up. They used their bayonets to snip off our shirt buttons. Before taking us away, they wanted us to take our clothes off to make sure we were not armed. Then, we heard the cocking of their rifles and we were sure we were going to be killed right there. After a long pause, they told us they just wanted to reload their weapons.

"At one point, I was ordered to drive a truck with a Japanese rider next to me. Another Japanese soldier was in front of the truck waving at me, directing me to back up. So I started backing up. Suddenly the rider next to me shouted and poked me in the ribs with his rifle. I stopped immediately. The soldier in front shouted and waved at me again. So I started backing up again and the rider shouted at me and poked me again. I was so confused. I finally learned that their hand gesture of waving meant to come forward rather than to go backwards.

"Eventually, I was separated from Woody and Zane. For one long day I was alone with the Japanese. They gave me a kind of saddle to sit on. There were a whole group of officers interrogating me. The only armed forces on the Island when war broke out were the Marines and the Navy. The Japanese asked me why I was wearing a Marine uniform. A lot of us at base had been given Marine clothing but—without the insignias. We worked in them. Part of this interrogation was to decide how to classify a person. They finally decided that since I was a civilian worker wearing Marines' clothing, I would be classified as a 'military civilian,' not eligible for exchange.

"Later I learned through the whisper of our interpreters that if the interrogators discovered any civilian had taken up arms, they would have been shot and I should have considered myself lucky as hell given all the dynamiting I had just done."

Germany and Italy reportedly had prior treaties with Japan whereby they would declare war on anyone threatening Japan. Consequently, the United States had little choice but to respond with a triple declaration of war against Japan, Germany, and Italy.[9,10] This would mean a tough break

---

[9] *The Library of Congress World War II Companion.* (2007). NY: Simon and Schuster, 113.
[10] http://www.law.yale.edu/library/3312.asp

for Ed. Suddenly, the United States had her hands full and she was simply not going to be able to rescue him "tomorrow" like he hoped.

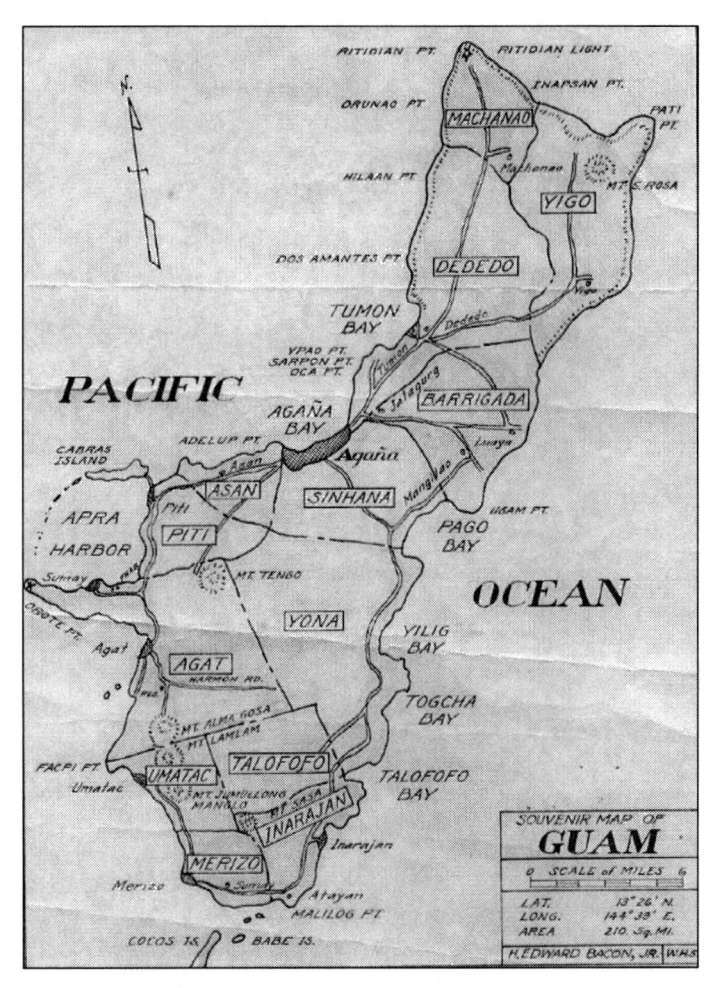

Souvenir Map of Guam found among Ed's keepsakes.

Ed and the other civilian contractors were held on Guam for over a month, incarcerated at a cathedral in Agana. They were fed one tablespoon of stew and a quarter of a potato a day to keep them weak, so they would be little trouble for the captors. To top it off they were made to hike every morning starting at 6 a.m. My father recalled growing weak and thin and even finding himself, on occasion, passing out. He also remembered something very strange during this first round of systematic starvation. For the rest of the month of December, he did not urinate.

The older we kids got, the more we learned of my father's experiences. Because he was never a heavy drinker it was rare to hear him reminisce "under the influence." But on one such rare occasion it became clear that those early days of his captivity held some of his darkest memories. One evening after several glasses of wine at my sister's home he began confidently recalling one of those hiking exercises in Agana during which one of the hungry prisoners reached out to grab an apple off an orchard tree and was instantly shot and killed in front of him. He went on to describe another incident in which several men—many who had been his friends—were shot in front of open graves into which they then fell. Forgetting the affect alcohol has on deep-seeded memories my father suddenly broke down weeping unable to continue.

Zentsuji: Ed's First Internment

PRISONERS ARE ADDRESSED BY A MAJOR-GENERAL OF THE JAPANESE FORCES WHO CLEARLY SPELLS OUT THEIR INCARCERATION.

One month after being captured, Ed became one of hundreds of American military and civilian personnel in Guam who were loaded onto the Argentina *Maru* and taken to Japan. Their first stop in Japan was Zentsuji Prisoner of War Camp.

Zentsuji sits strategically on the west side of Shikoku Island in southern Japan. Ed and others with him were some of the first prisoners in early 1942 brought to Zentsuji. Many prisoners were held there for years. Zentsuji appears to have warranted both good and bad accounts. During his capture, my father kept a diary, describing the internment camps he was moved in and out of. Of all the camps, Zentsuji was the worst.

When Ed arrived, it was cold and snowing. He remembered being cattled in with 75 fellow civilian contractors and hundreds of Marine and Navy personnel. And while he was only at Zentsuji for a short time, he recalled being hungry and cold, and having to sleep on the floor. Many of the men Ed saw there were suffering from flu and pneumonia as well.

> Instructions Given to The American Marines
> by Major-General Mizuhara,
> Superindentent of The Zentsuji War
> Prisoners' Camp,
> on the 15th day of January, 1942.

[It is requested that you should preserve these papers after having read them]

I am Major-General Mizuhara, Superintendent of the Zentsuji War Prisoners' Camp. Receiving you American marines here, I should like to give some instructions to you all.

You were faithful to your own country; you fought bravely; and you were taken captive unfortunately. As a warrior, belonging to the Imperial Army, I could not help expressing the profoundest sympathy and respect toward you.

I hope you will consider how this Greater East Asia War happened. To preserve the peace of the Pacific had always been the guiding principle of Japan's foreign policy, and the Japanese Government conducted patiently and prudently for eight long months diplomatic negotiations with the United States, endeavouring toward a peaceful solution, however ——— increased military preparations on all sides of the Japanese Empire to challenge us. The very existence of our nation being in danger, we stood up resolutely with a unity will strong as iron under our Sovereign to eliminate forever the sources of evil in East Asia.

Original 1942 text of General Mizuhara's instructions to captured Allied and American prisoners of war at Zentsuji.

It was at Zentsuji that Ed and the other prisoners received their first instructions from a high-ranking Japanese official. The address also served as a Japanese explanation of their captivity and the rationale for the war. It included references to the "Greater East Asian War," a phrase said to be banned by Western countries because it espoused Japan's version of the war's origin. A copy of the text was given to the prisoners and is the only souvenir Ed cared to keep of Zentsuji.

The following is the full text of the address taken from my father's original copy given to him at Zentsuji Prison on a cold winter day in 1942.

*Instructions Given to the American Marines
by Major-General Mizuhara,
Superintendent of the Zentsuji War
Prisoners' Camp,
on the 15th day of January 1942*

*(It is requested that you should preserve these
papers after having read them.)*

I am Major-General Mizuhara, Superintendent of the Zentsuji War Prisoners' Camp. Receiving you American Marines here, I should like to give some instructions to you all.

You were faithful to your own country; you fought bravely; and you were taken captive unfortunately. As a warrior, belonging to the imperial Army, I could not help expressing the profoundest sympathy and respect toward you.

I hope you will consider how this Greater East Asian War happened. To preserve the peace of the Pacific had always been the guiding principle of Japan's foreign policy, and the Japanese Government conducted patiently and prudently for eight long months diplomatic negotiations with the United States, endeavoring towards a peaceful settlement, while America and Britain increased military preparations on all sides of the Japanese Empire to challenge us. The very existence of our nation being in danger, we stood up resolutely with a unity of will strong as iron under our Sovereign to eliminate forever the sources of evil in East Asia. The rise or fall of Our Empire that has the glorious history of 3,000 years and the progress or decline of East Asia depend upon the present war. Firm and unshakable is our national resolve that we should crush our enemy, The United States of America and the British Empire.

Heaven is always on the side of Justice. Within three days after the War Declaration, our Navy annihilated both the American Pacific Fleet and the British Far Eastern Fleet; within one month, our Army captured Hong Kong and the Philippine Islands; and now the greater part of British Malaya have already been occupied by our Army, Singapore being on the verge of capitulation and Dutch East Indies, too, have been suffering several surprise attacks by our landing forces since the 11th day of this month.

In the Pacific arena there is left not a single battleship ... to the Allied Powers: Above our land there has appeared [not] a single aircraft belonging to them since the outbreak of the war, their air forces having been utterly crushed everywhere. Who can doubt this is the most brilliant success that has ever been recorded in the world history of war?

About the significance of the present war, I hope you will reconsider deeply with the clairvoyant calmness of mind that you must have acquired after the life and death struggle.

Next I should like to explain some principles as to how we shall treat you and how you should behave yourselves.

1. Though treating you strictly in accord with the regulations of our Army, we will make every effort to maintain your honor of being warriors, and your persons shall be fully under fair protection.

2. You should behave yourselves strictly in accordance with the discipline of the Japanese Imperial Army. Otherwise you will be severely punished according to the Martial Law.

3. As far as Japan is concerned, you must do away with the false superiority-complex idea that you seem to have been entertaining toward the Asiatic peoples. You should obey me and other Officers of the Japanese Army.

4. Prejudice against labor and grumbling over food, clothing and housing are strictly prohibited. ... We are now launching death-defying attacks on the Anglo-American military preparations in East Asia....There is not a single man or woman who is idling about in this country: Everyone is working as hard as possible in order to attain the aim of the present campaign.

Therefore, you must regard it as natural that you should not be allowed to be loose and reckless in your living. You ought to work as hard as the people of this country do.

5. Don't be demoralized; and do take good care of yourselves. As long as this war continues, your present mode of living will remain as it is. In order to endure this mode of living you should encourage each other in avoiding demoralization and taking good care of yourselves. Don't fail to hold the hope that peace will be recovered in the future and you will be allowed to return to your homes. I have ordered our medical officers to offer enough medical treatments to you in case you should be taken ill.

6. Among you officers and men of the American Marines you must maintain discipline. Be obedient to your seniors; be grateful to your juniors. None of you must bring disgrace upon the American Navy's glory.

7. If you should have any trouble in your personal affairs, don't refrain from telling our officers of them.

With the deepest sympathy with you as captives, I and our Officers will be pleased to be consulted with and will make every effort to alleviate your pain. Trust me and our Officers.

Closing my instructions, I advise you all to study Japanese language. I wish you to master it in the degree that you will not feel much inconvenienced in every-day conversations and

> *I hope you will be able to establish friendly relations between Japan and America when peace is restored in the future.*
>
> *(The End)*

All my father could think about at this point was that when he boarded the *USS Matsoni* in San Francisco, he sure as hell didn't sign up for this. Nor was he in the mood to be cheerful and learn a language as the camp director was suggesting. Quite the contrary! This kind of speech given after the humiliation of being captured would likely resurrect the Ricky Racer of his youth, the defiance of his younger days before the hallowed halls of Montezuma took to reshaping his soul.

After this presentation, Ed sat more like a cornered, angry, and bristled porcupine than the docile student-prisoner the camp director was hoping for. However, the general did urge the prisoners not once but twice to "take good care of yourselves"—a skill my father had been honing since childhood and would have no arguments crafting in every imaginable way he could think of.

The address serves as a reminder that for quite some time to come, Ed would continue to see and hear of the war through the Japanese perspective. Fortunately for Ed, within less than ten days, officials decided to at least move the civilians in his group north and out of Zentsuji.

Seaman's Mission:
Ed's Second Internment

ED IS MOVED TO KOBE'S SEAMAN'S MISSION AND NEARLY KILLS A GOOD FRIEND. MEANWHILE, NEWS OF HIS WHEREABOUTS IS REACHING HOME.

※◎❀◎※

On January 23, 1942, Ed was shipped out of Zentsuji and sent to Ivet's home city of Kobe, where he was first interned at Seaman's Mission. The group of civilians Ed was sent with was divided into two groups, older and younger men. The older men were sent to a different camp while the rest stayed at Seaman's. At least two of those staying with Ed were familiar faces, Woody and Zane. Captured as well was another U.S. civilian by the name of James Thomas, who'd served as assistant station manager for Pan American airlines, which had a base in Guam.

In his book *Trapped with the Enemy*, Thomas described his first impressions of Kobe's Seaman's Mission:

> The Mission was not an architect's dream. Dull, gray walls, dreary gables, small barred windows, cracked tile roof, and no sidewalk setback made the place look lonesome for companionship. Despite its looks, the room arrangements were functional and practical. Best of all, it had inside plumbing, beds and a potbellied stove, rare and

luxurious necessities. A living-dining room, with shelves of books, tables, chairs, the stove and a battered piano, greeted us as we entered. A small kitchen was hidden in the rear. Various sleeping rooms, hallways and alcoves were scattered throughout each floor.

Throughout the Orient, Seaman's Missions were owned and operated by the British government for the benefit of their merchant mariners—a sailor's refuge away from home. Equipped with beds, kitchens and libraries, these establishments were enclaves of tranquility in foreign lands. This particular mission was intended to accommodate about twenty persons in relative comfort, not a crowd of seventy-four homesick derelicts, bone tired and mentally paralyzed. Psychiatrists would have wondered how we avoided claustrophobic nightmares. We didn't have the luxury of self-pity so we bit the proverbial bullet and thought of food, home and freedom.[11]

It was still snowing and cold when the men arrived in Kobe. Without his usual grooming or diet, Ed was becoming thinner and unkempt as well as being down to his last $5.00. The cold and crowded conditions were enough to put anyone in a perpetually bad mood. Add to that hunger, and tensions could easily escalate even among friends.

Ed recalled that the last piece of a loaf came to be considered gold because there is, texturally, a higher concentration of dough captured in the back of the slice. Not surprising, one dinner erupted in a brawl. Ed and Zane, whom he'd jokingly scrapped with in Guam (remember the lost mustache?), found themselves at each other's throats over a slice of bread. These were two hefty guys whose common interest in high school was tackle football. They had lost some weight but were still quite capable of sending tables and chairs, forks and knives flying every which way and giving new meaning to the phrase *Mess Hall*. But this time they weren't joking. "It was a slice of bread and we damn near killed each other."

---

[11] Thomas, J. O. *Trapped with the Enemy*, Xlibris, 97-98.

Years prior, Ed had worked the graveyard shift in the dripping Golden Gate Tunnel and stared out at the city lights of San Francisco imagining people in their warm homes. One wonders how often he stared out of the gloomy Seamen's Mission to get a glimpse of something to hope for in the snow-laden city of Kobe of January 1942. San Francisco was attainable from the hills of Sausalito, the temporary draw of a cold night shift. This was a much harder reality that is notably absent in his diaries. A cruel twist of fate had taken him from the idyllic scenes of the South Pacific to a crowded cage, unkempt, half-starved, and scrapping over a piece of bread. My father was a proud man and this was, no doubt, a particularly humiliating time for him.

Within a couple of months, news of the American captives reached the mainland. A February 19 edition of *The San Francisco News* dedicated a full page to those "believed to be prisoners of Japan." The page carried a photo of Ed as well as listing Stubbe and Woody as among those taken from Guam. My grandmother Lucylle was also receiving news from the United Press and the War Department.

Ed always referred to Lucylle as "Mother." We knew her as *Grandma*. She was proper and stern in the upbringing of children and grandchildren, but she could also be admiring and engaging. She was always "dressed to the nines," cigarette in hand and perfumed. When I came home from school, I could tell when Grandma was visiting. Her royal presence preceded her. *Bellodgia* perfume mixed with the sweet smell of tobacco permeated the house.

She wore dark purple hand-knit dresses, black high heels, red lipstick and fingernail polish, diamond rings, and white-rimmed glasses, and her wavy silk-white hair topped her off at 5'5". Even her apartment garden—only a mile from us—was designed with the rich dark colors of primroses and purple violets. If you pointed at something, you were never to use one finger, always two. A woman holds a cane with the curved handle facing her while a man grabs the cane with the curve facing outward. And balloons were not welcomed at the dinner table to which the tip of her cigarette accented her point.

Grandma also tutored me once during a series of weekends and was single-handedly responsible for teaching me how to memorize the times tables while she sat and knit and desperately tried to remember to stop crossing her nylon ankles per her doctor's instructions. Wherever she was in 1942, one can be sure her richly carpeted apartment had a quietly ticking clock, an elegant dressing room, satin-striped upholstered chairs, sterling silver cigarette lighters, gold-plated pens and telephone notepads—all absorbed in a colloquy of the warm fragrances of rich perfume, tobacco, and brewed coffee. And all of which was soon to be interrupted by the chilling news of her son.

In a March 1942 letter addressed to Lucylle, the United Press informed Grandma that they had intercepted a Japanese broadcast that seemed to reference her son. UP made it clear that they had not heard the broadcast but merely transcribed the message. But as Lucylle slowly read the text of the letter, everything became frighteningly familiar. Ed's name spelled out just like his birth certificate, his age, his mention of Marjorie and, last but not least, Lucylle's street address. Grandma suddenly knew how that lightning bolt felt that had killed her father: a horrid twist grabbed the pit of her stomach sending her to a chair while she forced herself to read on, taking in Ed's explanations as to where he was.

1945. "Grandma" Bacon waited over three years for her son's return.

His reassurances that he was okay fell painfully short for Lucylle as she learned he had been captured and shipped to Japan. Finally, any lingering doubts as to the authenticity of the message were settled by Ed's characteristically self-deprecating closing apology: "Sorry I didn't get your Christmas presents to you." Ed knew what his plight would mean to his mother. He was desperate to leave her smiling with such an apology as he reluctantly doomed her to years of worry.

In April, Lucylle received a letter from the War Department as well, which had intercepted essentially the same message. So, while the earlier *San Francisco News* article hinted at Ed's capture in February, by April these new sources confirmed for Lucylle the true whereabouts of her son. It had been four months since she had last heard from him.

About this time, the Seaman's Mission received their first call from the Swiss Consulate. Both the Swiss Consulate and the Unity Church brought monetary gifts to the men. Ed received the equivalent of $25 from the two groups. This became a turning point. Ed's anger was beginning to "level off" as the monetary gifts lifted his spirits. He also seemed to be taking advantage of the Mission's small library, which proved a good diversion and a catalyst that stirred up dreams of his future that had, up to now, been fully abandoned. Soon Ed wrote a letter home. It was the first written expression of optimism from him in five months.

> *... When you hear of me coming home, be sure to have one of those pies and cakes waiting for me .... If I get the money from the Contractors I am going to buy or build a poultry ranch when I get back. I have a chance to do some studying up on it and there is a very good chance to make money.*

Meanwhile, war pressed on. In Europe, mass executions of Jews were beginning to take place in Auschwitz. In the United States, Japanese Americans were being sent to Relocation Centers. And, in Japan the United States was taking its first aim with the infamous Doolittle Raids. The Doolittle Raids had American fighter planes not only launching missions off a ship, which did not normally launch B-25s, but the ship was not designed for the planes to return onboard either. Consequently, the fighter pilots had to later land somewhere in China.[12] It was, without a doubt, an unusual and courageous endeavor in the eyes of Americans. One of the Doolittle raids occurred very close to the Seaman's Mission. Ed recalled the bombing in a brief diary entry.

April 18, 1942. First bombing here in Kobe by U.S. Navy @ 3 p.m. Fires broke out a few blocks from us.

While my father was showing signs of coping for the first time by reading, dreaming about his future, and even bothering to chronicle Kobe's first air raid, one would expect the memory of Arlene—arguably the reason he was a captive in the first place—to be the farthest thing from his mind. And yet throughout all this, Ed managed to take special note of one important anniversary in a gleeful diary entry.

---

[12] *The Library of Congress World War II Companion.* (2007). NY: Simon & Schuster, 508-510.

April 22, 1942. ****Divorce Final****

Ed and Arlene had been granted a divorce in the spring of 1941 but one that stipulated a waiting period followed by a formal court decision. While the waiting period had been satisfied, a formal court decision had never been petitioned or granted. Neither Ed nor Arlene had followed up. Unfortunately, it was a small oversight that would later come to haunt Ed.

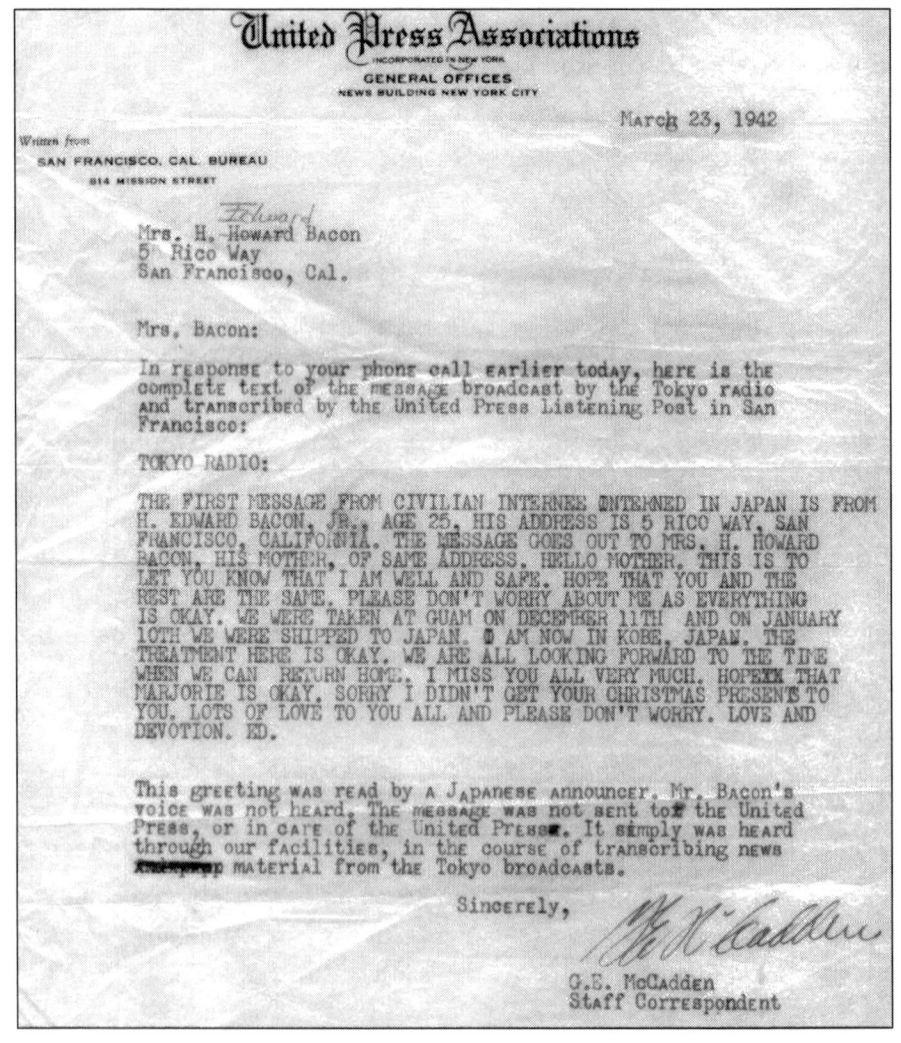

> **United Press Associations**
> INCORPORATED IN NEW YORK
> GENERAL OFFICES
> NEWS BUILDING NEW YORK CITY
>
> March 23, 1942
>
> Written from:
> SAN FRANCISCO, CAL. BUREAU
> 814 MISSION STREET
>
> Mrs. H. ~~Howard~~ *Edward* Bacon
> 5 Rico Way
> San Francisco, Cal.
>
> Mrs. Bacon:
>
> In response to your phone call earlier today, here is the complete text of the message broadcast by the Tokyo radio and transcribed by the United Press Listening Post in San Francisco:
>
> TOKYO RADIO:
>
> THE FIRST MESSAGE FROM CIVILIAN INTERNEE INTERNED IN JAPAN IS FROM H. EDWARD BACON, JR., AGE 25. HIS ADDRESS IS 5 RICO WAY, SAN FRANCISCO, CALIFORNIA. THE MESSAGE GOES OUT TO MRS. H. HOWARD BACON, HIS MOTHER, OF SAME ADDRESS. HELLO MOTHER. THIS IS TO LET YOU KNOW THAT I AM WELL AND SAFE. HOPE THAT YOU AND THE REST ARE THE SAME. PLEASE DON'T WORRY ABOUT ME AS EVERYTHING IS OKAY. WE WERE TAKEN AT GUAM ON DECEMBER 11TH AND ON JANUARY 10TH WE WERE SHIPPED TO JAPAN. I AM NOW IN KOBE, JAPAN. THE TREATMENT HERE IS OKAY. WE ARE ALL LOOKING FORWARD TO THE TIME WHEN WE CAN RETURN HOME. I MISS YOU ALL VERY MUCH. HOPE THAT MARJORIE IS OKAY. SORRY I DIDN'T GET YOUR CHRISTMAS PRESENTS TO YOU. LOTS OF LOVE TO YOU ALL AND PLEASE DON'T WORRY. LOVE AND DEVOTION. ED.
>
> This greeting was read by a Japanese announcer. Mr. Bacon's voice was not heard. The message was not sent to the United Press, or in care of the United Press. It simply was heard through our facilities, in the course of transcribing news material from the Tokyo broadcasts.
>
> Sincerely,
>
> G.E. McCadden
> Staff Correspondent

1942. United Press Associations sends a copy of a communiqué to my grandmother regarding Ed's whereabouts. After three months since Ed's disappearance, this is Lucylle's first real evidence that her son had been captured.

Marks House: Ed's Third Internment

*A*FTER 10 MONTHS ED HEARS FROM HOME FOR THE FIRST TIME. THE PRISONERS ARE ALSO MOVED AGAIN BRINGING ED EVEN CLOSER TO A CHANCE ENCOUNTER WITH A YOUNG TURKISH GIRL FROM KOBE.

While they still had not met, Ed and Ivet were living only miles away from each other by the fall of 1942 and in a country that was a homeland to neither one of their families. Ivet's family had immigrated with their Tatar community from western Russian, on what might be called an epic journey for a place they could call their home, while traveling and trading among the Asiatic worlds on the way. Ed brought his family footprints from New York State across the prairie hills of the Midwest to San Francisco, and now across the Pacific to the very doorstep of that Tatar family.

In June of 1942, my mother was 18 and had graduated from school. She spent that summer in nearby Shioya as a governess to a French Consul, taking care of his three daughters. It was also during this time when she took on the French version of her name. In Shioya, Effie met many European friends and began introducing herself as *Ivet*. She fondly recalled that summer.

"During this time, I was a member of the Shioya Country Club. On my days off, I had time to enjoy the social activities. They had a beautiful beach and night dances. They also had swimming events between two other clubs. At one of the meets, I had the pleasure of winning one of the races and a cup for our club."

Perhaps those races served her well as Ivet would soon find herself in a different kind of race. A race against time as an ugly war slowly approached and would soon eclipse the happy hills of Japan that Ivet had grown accustomed to.

Meanwhile, in downtown Kobe, Ed paced the floors of the Seaman's Mission for the next hopeful visit from the Swiss Consul and took a sneak shot of a whiskey bottle. He celebrated his birthday in a diary entry, peppered with cynicism.

July 27th ... It's my birthday today. I got out and got drunk. Also caught by the guards. The rest I can't remember very well. Although last week I shaved for the first time in 8 months. I had quite a beard. The Swiss Consul stopped by this month and last month. $70 in total. Today also ends my contract with PNAB, which they will no doubt give me a good screwing on.

After nearly eight months of imprisonment, who wouldn't get drunk? My father was never a heavy drinker. In fact, he was hardly a drinker at all. He used to admit quite frankly that he never liked alcohol, even beer. So this was actually a good sign. He wasn't drinking because he had been beaten down or to anesthetize himself; this was more impetuous and rebellious. It was a positive, to-hell-with-this-situation-I'm-celebrating attitude. He would tease and say he was just following the Superintendent's instructions "not to be demoralized!" The point is, his spirit was alive and that was a good thing and it would soon be put to truly good use.

Another good thing that was coming out of the waning summer of '42 for Ed and the rest of his fellow POWs: letters and telegrams were beginning to get through. Even a transcript of Zane's broadcast earlier in the year found its way into Herb Caen's column in the *San Francisco Chronicle*:

> *... And the other night, that soft-voiced [Tokyo Rose] was broadcasting via short wave from Tokyo and she gave the names of various American prisoners. Then on came a San*

Franciscan named Zane A. Stickel of 70 Cedro Way, who said he was a civilian defense worker captured at Guam—and he hoped someone listening would phone Delaware 6838 and tell his mother he was alright and hoped to be home soon ....[13]

Later, the fall of 1942 ushered in an even more significant change. After a 10-month stint at the Seaman's Mission, Ed and 50 other prisoners were moved to a place called the Marks House. It was a move of mixed emotions for the internees but one that would prove to be the epicenter of this particular East/West romance.

Marks House Prisoners of War, 1943. Named after the previous owner whose house was confiscated in order to house POWs. Middle row and third from the left, my father, **H. Edward Bacon**. Third row from the bottom and third from the right, **Arthur (Woody) Woodruff.** Zane is absent having been sent earlier to the Canadian Academy.

Fifty of us are moving into the former residence of a Mr. Marks at No. 20 Yamamoto-dori, 2 chome (3 blocks from Butterfield) and the other 24 to the Canadian Academy, Woody recounted in his diary.[14]

---

[13] Caen, H. (March 1942). *San Francisco Chronicle.*
[14] Arthur Woodruff diary.

The Marks House was a large private Kobe residence that the Japanese simply confiscated in order to house their growing number of prisoners. It was one of hundreds of prisoner of war locales throughout Japan as the war grew. The significance of the Marks House is that it happened to be only blocks from a food rations center—one that would serve Ivet's neighborhood as the war escalated.

This large secured residence would end up being home for Ed for the next 18 months: 50 men, along with 7 guards, squeezed into one house with a 25 x 75-foot exercise yard. There were 9 men in Ed's room—the size of an average bedroom.

Next door to the Marks House lived the Sidline family. George Sidline, the younger of the two boys, was 7 years old when the prisoners occupied the Marks House. In his recent book *Somehow, We'll Survive,* George recalled both the mundane and mysterious activities of his next-door neighbors:

> From our vantage point at the upstairs bedroom window, we observed the activity in the camp. There did not seem to be any specific routine; mostly monotony and boredom. The prisoners had a windup phonograph on which they played the few records that somehow the Americans acquired. Those who felt like it played ball or exercised. Occasionally, some of the senior guard officers would bring their families, and we could see their children playing in the yard. There were no obvious atrocities committed here like in other camps where downed flyers were imprisoned, tortured and often executed, as was reported after the war. The arrival of the food truck was the daily highlight. The food came in a large drum containing a weak gruel and not much else. Definitely not enough to maintain proper health and nutrition for the young men there. Disease and weight loss were the rule.
>
> The front of our house was set back from the road by a courtyard. A small inner gate that we locked every night blocked external access to the space between our house and the wall of the Marks yard. One morning on our way out, we noticed the gate unlocked. We thought nothing of it,

assuming that we had merely forgotten to lock it the night before. When it happened again, my parents became suspicious. Over the next few weeks, from time to time, we found the gate unlocked. We finally realized that under cover of darkness, some of the prisoners hopped over the wall into our yard and went downtown. Later that night they would come back into our yard and quietly slip over the wall back into the camp.[15]

As time went on, the Sidline family secretly befriended the prisoners and smuggled food to them when they could.

At the Marks House, these men would learn to cope with hunger, boredom, rats, and even indigenous monkeys, in ways one might say only skilled, cunning, and ingenious American tradesmen would. Still, as George Sidline noted, Ed and the others were lucky. There were many POW camps in Japan far worse off. The Marks House detained civilians and therefore was not a "labor" camp, although hunger and disease remained prevalent.

By the autumn of 1942, those letters from home began arriving as did more packages from the Red Cross, the Swiss Consul, and monetary gifts from the Vatican and the Unity Church. Nearly 10 months after being captured, Ed finally heard from his family. Life could have been worse. But it could have been better. Ed leaves 1942 with a simple diary entry:

December 25, Christmas in a prison.

---

[15]Sidline, G. *Somehow, We'll Survive.* Portland, OR: Vera Vista Publishing, 81-82.

84 • Ed & Ivet

Marks House backyard, 1944. Top L-R: Joe Hermes, Bill Smith, Bill Gordanier, Halsey Meyer, Herb Mead, Bob Hoffstot, Walt Pleitner, Jim O'Leary. Middle L-R: Ken Fraser, Roy Henning, Art Occhipinti, Ken Hardy. Above Hardy: **Ed Bacon**, Harold Wickman, Bill Falvey, Bob Aitken, Woody Ashby, Charles Moneyhun, **Art Woodruff**, Larry Neass, Frank Rupert, Leon Harris, Ken Meyer, Tom Apedaile., Cecil, Downing, Neil Campbell. Bottom L-R: Frank Angell, Bill Young, Gus Gilbert, Jack Taylor, Doc McNulty, Gene Clary, Bryant Sterling, Tiny Lucke, Nick Enerti, Don Wallace, Ed Maxim, Harry Burrow, Alton White. The back fence was heightened in an effort to discourage smuggling.

> Kobe, Japan
> May 22, 1942.
>
> Mrs. H. Edward Bacon
> 5 Rico Way
> San Francisco, California,
> USA
>
> Dearest Mother and Family:
>
> We have been permitted to write a short letter home.
>
> I'm O.K. and in good health, so please don't worry about me. I miss you all very much and would give anything to be home with you now. When you do hear of me coming home, be sure to have one of those pies and cakes waiting for me. I sure do miss them.
>
> If I get the money from the Contractors, I am going to buy or build a poultry ranch when I get back. I have had a chance to do some studying up on it and there is a very good chance to make good money in it.
>
> Say Hello to everyone for me. We do not know how long we will be here but when the day comes it will be a happy one.
>
> Please save this letter if you do get it. I sure hope that you are all well and safe. I'm thinking of you all every day. My love to all of you and hope that it won't be long before we are together again.
>
> With love and devotion,
>
> H Edward Bacon, Jr.

1942. Ed's first letter home reveals that while he understands his future is uncertain, his dreams are still alive.

1943: Diaries and Letters

The pen can be both revealing and evasive especially when it comes to hardship. Hardship is working its way up the hills of Kobe as well, priming an imminent meeting.

※

During 1943 Ed wrote many letters home, and we get an understanding of some of his frustrations in this second year of captivity. One underlying frustration is that while he is sending letters, he is getting nothing in return. He was also careful to separate the anger and frustration found in his diary and he used more optimistic and sometime contradictory tones in his letters home.

For instance, Christmas of '42, as recalled in his diary, was ho-hum. The earlier Red Cross boxes he'd received were noted as simply *some stuff*. And yet when writing home he describes those same boxes as *grand Christmas presents*. Likewise, in a February letter home, he tells his mother his *health is good, everything fine, cheer up, and don't worry*. Yet two weeks later his diary revealed this: *In all the time we have been here we have received no clothing from either the Swiss Consul or the Red Cross. I have been wearing the same pr of contractor's shoes that I had in Guam.*

His diary goes on to agonize, *one year as a prisoner, seems like ten,* while in the next letter home he tells his family to *cheer up. This won't last forever ....*

The diary allowed Ed to vent but to do so privately. And that was important, for Ed was the kind of guy who could, at times, turn the air blue with his wisecracks. Under these circumstances he could not afford to do that. The diary and letters consistently portray a dual personality. The diary reveals an individual under pressure and is, consequently, critical and sometimes offensively sarcastic and more revealing. On the other hand, the letters take him home where he regains a more cordial, generous, and optimistic nature. This is not just because the letters were being censored, but because my father was not the kind of person who would want to further burden his mother with reports of his poor health. Some of these contrasts in his writings are found early in 1943 beginning with his rather salty diary entries.

Jan 1st New Years and still here. Why doesn't Uncle Sam blast the hell out of these #$@* and get the thing over with?

Jan 8th During all the time we've been here, the Red Cross called on us just once last March. Once in one year. If the Red Cross ever asks for $ of me again they can go plumb to hell. At the time [the Representative] said he'd let the States know how well off we were. If he calls it "well off," I guess he has lived in the gutter all his life.

April 23rd I've changed my mind about Oakland. It's a grand place after all.

June 30th So far this year I have been stung by a scorpion once on the shoulder, bitten on the arm and leg by a monkey, and bitten on the hand by a rat. This place is lousy with rats. We have killed as many as four in our room in one day. At night they run over the tops of the beds and being as hot as it is, we usually sleep with nothing over us. Several guys have been bitten. There are also centipedes and mosquitoes enough to drive one nuts.

July 8th 19 months and I am still wearing the same pr of shoes I had when captured ... I got one towel when captured and I am still using the same one ... We have had a total of 4 bars of lousy soap issued in 19 months. The last one was 3 months ago. I have 3 pr of socks but cannot wear them as I must save them for winter. When I was taken captive, I had 1 pr of shoes 1 pr of socks 1 pr of workpants and 1 work shirt. All I had to carry was the picture of mother and dad and my one and only towel. We are all in need of clothing very badly ... We have no overcoats and the winters are damn cold here.

The letters Ed wrote home during this same period of time carry a strikingly different tone.

Feb 23rd [To Mother] ... Do you still have the boys over for hot cakes on Mondays? Hope they find hunting good this year. Health good, everything fine, cheer up don't worry.

March 23rd [To Marjorie:] Thanks again for your letters [and] ... for paying Leo. I'll pay you back soon. Tell Joe I'm ready to come home. Hope I can make up for all the fine things you've done.

April 23rd [To Marjorie] ... Pictures mean so much. Please send more .... Health fine. Hope I'll be able to take you to dinner next year this time.

May 23rd [To Mother] ... If you can get money from Pomeroy [Ed's contractor in Guam] please use it. Take another trip. Have a good time. Hope to spend Xmas '44 home with family.

July 21st [To Marjorie] ... Health is fine. Hope my things I left in storage are still there. Do you see any of my friends anymore? ... Say hello to everyone. Uncle Sam is doing great.

There is simply no talk of dire needs in his letters home. Still, for all he knew, Ed might as well have been writing in a vacuum. As late as May of 1943, he wrote his mother that he had read her letters over and over even though, by now, they were a year old. In a number of letters, he repeated, *I have received nothing from home since October of '42.*

Likewise, on the other side of the Pacific, Lucylle sat pensive and alone in her San Francisco apartment. And while she listened to news that the Germans had attacked London and the Americans had taken Sicily, she thought of her own boy who was much too far away. One can almost hear the breath being sucked out of her trying to take comfort in patio plants as she wrote to him.

... Just finished a batch of cookies. Wish I could send some to you. Marjorie is away with her work so I am alone .... Well, you will soon have another

birthday. How I wish you could drop by and say hello to me. … The flowers in the patio are very lovely this year …. They've asked we make letters short, good night and my blessing upon you, my dear boy. Love, Mother

Ed received that letter six months later.

Again, what is striking was the vacuum both of them were writing in. While they were articulating their concerns and passions and hopes and fears, the letters were not being immediately received or answered. Their letters were like prayers—genuine concerns sent in hopes of being received. This was the case throughout 1943.

December 1943 letter to Ed. It often took months before Ed received letters from home.

Someone else who had taken to the pen was Ed's fellow internee, Woody. Woody's diary was very different from my father's. Besides being a voracious reader, Woody was "front and center" when it came to camp politics. Consequently, his diary covered many of the events in camp in great detail as well as an occasional book review. In time, the men were able to obtain outside news, which Woody followed religiously and which added to his commentary in addition to the chronicling of his personal thoughts. In fact, Woody had sets of diaries. They were voluminous.

On the other hand, my father's diary entries were short and to the point but more varied in nature. My father copied all the letters he sent home. He had a separate section on his personal daily thoughts. He also had a section that included bookkeeping and lists such as items in ration kits, important dates, and monetary exchange rates. His diary also coded and calendared events. My father's diary was thin enough to slide down his pants if he had to in a hurry. Woody's diaries practically needed a shelf, which soon proved problematic for him.

"Good things come to he who waits" and in late September Ed wrote home that he had finally received Lucylle's January letter of the same year. While Ed remained consistent in avoiding talk of his dire needs, he was always comfortable with a little sarcasm.

... Received mother's and Marjorie's letters of January 1943. Words fail to express what your letters mean to me. Marjorie asked if it was pretty over here. Haven't seen anything yet that was. My true sentiments are that it stinks .... Tell Mother not to forget how to make pies and cakes.

Unfortunately, by the fall of 1943, my father's dire needs had by no means ended, as he noted privately in his diary. Hunger was becoming a serious issue. He was losing more weight, it was getting cold, and a second internee had died. However, during this time he continued to write home that his health was good and for his family not to worry even though his diary entries were painting quite a different picture.

Oct 11th Johnson died at 2:30 pm today. He is the second one to die since we have been here in Kobe. It's a wonder that there haven't been a lot more.

Oct 15th Our first clothing issued since we have been here last year. 2 badly stained shirts and 2 pr of unmatched socks.

Oct 22nd Been out of coal now for 2 days. No breakfast this morning and none tomorrow. Looks like a bad winter for us. My weight is now 169 lbs. When I left Frisco I weighed 201 lbs. Not enough food to keep a bird healthy. Most of the food is so goddamn rotten one can't eat it. Rooster combs and chicken guts in the soup. Sea slugs, fish with head, scales, guts and all. Seaweed for greens. Worms in the rice. Sawdust and what is supposed to be bread. I could write ten pages on this alone.

Oct 29th Informed today that the Red Cross Rep has been interned also as a Prisoner of War. Fat chance we'll get help from them.

The worsening conditions at camp were not going unnoticed by the Japanese. Deterioration is never a good thing for captors and the last thing one wants to do is to complain too much to them, not to mention be found documenting sour conditions. There was tension in the air. And as the fall of '43 was setting in, Woody was becoming nervous over prying eyes. He found himself faced with a tortuous decision and soon confided in one of his diaries.

… the minor Japanese Authorities in charge of us began to take, shall we say, an undue interest in diaries, and because I had, in certain instances, set down little phrases which I felt might grate at their delicate eardrums and because of a certain eminence in Camp politics which was my lot at the time, the diaries disappeared in the kitchen stove—a thing which I've regretted very keenly ever since.

Fortunately, Woody had the skill, memory, and determination to draft a new journal at another time when things lightened up—which is precisely what he did.

As the war progressed, the prisoners were not the only ones facing scarcities. The civilian population in Japan had begun a rationing program as well by 1943. The rationings would ultimately draw residents from the hills downtown. One resident in particular would find herself curious about those American prisoners held at the Marks House as she walked by.

PART FOUR: ROMANCE

Ed and Ivet Meet

In the end, it is the hardships of war that ultimately bring Ed and Ivet together. Curiosity leads to compassion as Ivet breaches the secrecy of a prison fence.

※○○※

By the fall of 1943 Ed had been a prisoner for almost two years. In this changing climate, Ivet was called home from her governess job in Shioya. Both she and her parents wanted her home as the war grew more intense.

The war presented a then unknown paradox for Ed and Ivet. Neither of them wanted life in Japan to deteriorate further, but without that, they might never have met. This same sort of war-initiated paradox had happened to Ivet's parents. Safa and Maksura might never have come to their new life in Japan had they not felt the 1917 sting of the Russian civil war. In another sort of paradox, my grandfather Harry might never have arrived in San Francisco without the debilitating exhaustion of his Midwest practice. Good things don't always come out of bad situations, but sometimes they do.

It was while my father was at the Marks House that my parents first met. The Marks House was a three-story mansion with two enclosed porches. It had three bedrooms—three bedrooms—for the now 45 prisoners held there. The home had been owned by a British banker by the name of Marks, who had been repatriated. His home held American civilians and expatriates in addition to businessmen who had lived in Kobe.

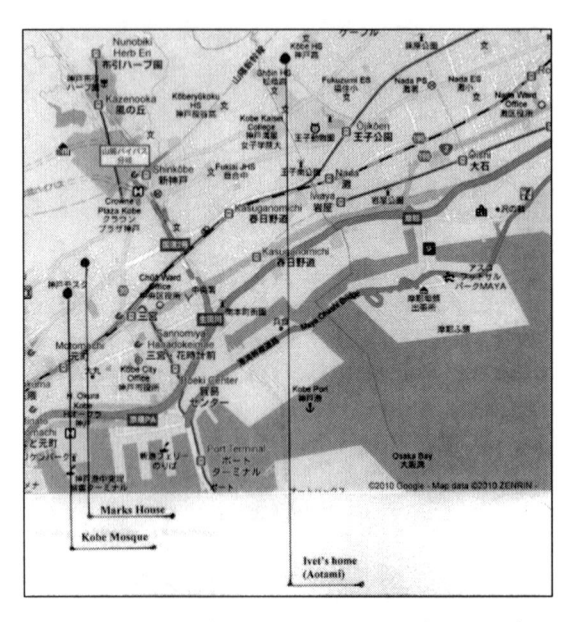

Marks House was located on Yamamoto dori with its entrance on Kitano-cho, streets my mother used on her way to get rations for her family who lived farther up the hill. As a young Effie, my mother may have skipped past the Marks House holding onto her mother's hand on their walks to downtown Kobe. Now, as a young adult, she walked with poise and a gentle air of sophistication. She was, after all, the fetching daughter of a seasoned Turkish actress and a successful tradesman, a good catch by all standards. And while one would not expect someone with those inherited traits to be painfully shy, my mother very often was.

It was a curious combination: here was someone who was—like my father—normally shy in social settings and yet quite capable of capturing attention if she needed to with keen instincts of what was and was not good for her, which, in turn, afforded her the occasional bold step in approaching someone. And certainly for Ed, it didn't hurt that all this was shrouded in starry-eyed optimistic generosity.

My mother had these memories of the day she met my father: "During the war when everything started to get scarce, the government started rationing, especially food. They divided food for each community. So much for the Tatar community, so much for the Italian community, the Russian community, and so forth. Our food center was in Hamate, which was in the downtown center of the city about 5 miles from our home. A lot of our people lived in the city. Our mosque was very close to the food center. Most of our people went to mosque every Friday. So it was convenient for people to pick up their food once or twice a week. Near the food center was this big house [Marks House], which the Japanese Army had turned into a prisoner camp to keep American POWs.

"Every so often I asked to go to the food center to pick up our rations. I was usually with cousins or my friends. On the way home, as we would pass Marks House, we became curious. We used to peek through the cracks of the fence and converse with the prisoners. I was very scared to be caught so I didn't do it too often, but my cousin Naila hung around all the time whenever she could.

"Still, when you're young, you keep doing foolish things. And we kept trying to talk with them. This was when I first met your dad. They were short conversations between the fence boards, on the way to get our rations. But I caught his eye and he caught mine."

The prisoners at Marks House were allowed a small backyard to roam in freely. Voices could be heard. As Ivet walked by, the slits of the wooden fence gave snapshots of those behind the muffled voices in the backyard. My mother was now 19 and my father was 28. She was a young Turkish Moslem girl, chaste and innocent, dedicated to her family and loyal to her faith. What made this meeting possible was that there was, like the slits in the fence, a slice of curiosity in the virtuous *Effat* that, no doubt, she inherited from her upstanding but risk-taking father Safa. Everything about my mother would normally have led her to keep walking, that that house was none of her business, that it was without question off limits to her, and that she should continue on her way. That respect for authority was genuine and is what made my mother *Effat*.

But like those openings in the fence, the rays of unconventional compassion in *Effat's* soul are what made her *Ivet*. Unlike my father's earlier intoxicated form of civil disobedience, my mother's version was much more subtle: lathered and blinded in love while persistent with a purity of heart. And this disobedience was not political in the traditional sense. She had little interest in politics. Rather, like an unfair wrestling match, her otherwise restrained curiosity could be easily overtaken by her more dominant sense of compassion, especially once she'd made her mind up. Because of her uncanny intuition, she could also make these decisions quickly. Unlike my father whose previous unrequited love left him "once burnt twice shy," my mother carried no emotional baggage and could size up my father in an instant, which may explain why this normally shy 19 year-old felt so comfortable approaching this tall American stranger.

The house on Yamamoto dori filled my mother with intrigue more and more as she approached each Friday until finally one day, the teasing fence revealed my father's gazing hazel eyes. With his bird's-eye view, Cupid took a clear shot. My mother didn't stand a chance, nor did my father. Ivet approached the fence. Her heavy accent charmed the air with enticing broken English while her natural smile, her long black glistening hair, and deep brown eyes took to my father like headlights to a deer. He returned the favor, as he would with any greeting stranger, with a coy smile that was equally disarming and sparing eye contact, which he used to signal he was nonthreatening. Except in this case she was not just any stranger and he found a gentleness about her that was reassuring, which seemed to allow him further eye contact. Occasionally, her hand reached to touch the fence while she kept a careful eye on the street. Sometimes he stood sideways looking down at his feet in an effort to also appear nonchalant from any distant glance of the guards. Gradually their meetings increased with a peculiar romantic tension for while they grew to cherish these brief encounters, exposure of any kind could not only end the relationship but bring on unknown consequences to either one of them.

As I look back, I can't help admire that my parents met in such foreboding circumstances. It not only speaks of the resiliency of love but that while they both respected authority, in time, they both proved determined to challenge everything that wooden fence represented in order to be together.

The Fence. The backyard photo of the Marks House POWs captures the barely visible narrow slits in the fence where my parents first met. While hardly private, the scene was the genesis of their lifelong relationship.

Ivet's concern over Ed's plight grew and soon she began smuggling food to him regularly. In the beginning, it was small items. Taking the batteries out of a flashlight and filling it with food stuffs became an easy way to get things through the fence. The exchange quickly grew to books, small cooking utensils, black market items, more food, and much later—stolen kisses.

As the war grew heavier, Maksura stopped letting Ivet go out so it became harder for Ivet to see Ed. While it became harder, it was, however, not impossible and Ivet would later find clever ways of getting goods to Ed and the others.

Throughout the chilly fall, Ed continued to write home to family and friends stirring up memories and conversations with them in an effort to cope with an increasingly harsh reality. Marks House was a big house in a nice neighborhood. But it was still crowded, they suffered from rodents, and the food was terrible. In diary entries Ed berated the cold and mosquitoes that *eat the hell out of us every night.* He noted the sudden transfer of prisoners, an occasional knife fight, friends dying in sick bay, and the desperate ongoing wish for food, clothing, and American air raids that would *get it all over with.*

Eventually all his wishes would come true. In the meantime, his writings continued like two sets of drums. His diary played hard, facing the reality around him while letters home entertained the imaginary, planned future endeavors, recalled past hay days, recreated family photos, and tasted his mother's cakes and pies.

The difference now was that in his real world of harsh realities someone new had emerged in brief and secret conversations: a charming and sympathetic girl who did not live in his unseen imagination across the Pacific but, in fact, just up the hill only miles from his imprisonment. Now, unlike the stark days of the Seaman's Mission, Ed at least had something to look forward to within his reach—someone to look forward to. There is nothing like love that strengthens the soul and diminishes the pulse of prolonged anxiety—nature's anti-depressant—to give a person vision, purpose, and direction. Such an unexpected tonic is lucky to be found in peacetime much less in the second year of one's internment. But judging by his first marriage, Ed was no doubt still leery of the "joys" of love. His proud Leo heart would now need to sense genuine consideration beneath a catching smile. Fortunately, Ivet would prove to fit the bill. She was a stereotypical "hot" Mother Teresa and, frankly, it was an image that didn't change much throughout her life.

And so Ed and Ivet met for the first time—in the autumn of 1943. Ed, thirty pounds skinnier than when he'd left the States, locked up in a large house packed with other prisoners and anxious over the thoughts of an approaching winter. And Ivet, young and curious and busy with her family's rations, yet finding herself drawn to the plight of a tall, hungry, incarcerated American and in a city that had already experienced American bombings and that sat less than 200 miles from Hiroshima.

Couples meet in a thousand different ways. This was how my parents met: a forbidden encounter through a fence during a world war. In some ways, this was not surprising. They were, after all, separated by so many things already: politics, geography, tradition, religion. They were speaking through so many fences. But those fences would, one by one, be dissolved by love.

> *Something there is that doesn't love a wall,*
> *That wants it down.* – Robert Frost

Another Romance: Naila and Woody

L OVE STEALTHS ANOTHER ARROW. ED AND IVET ARE NOT THE ONLY COUPLE STRIKING UP A SECRET ROMANCE AT MARKS HOUSE.

~~~~~~

A s Ivet mentioned, she was usually with her cousins or her friends on her way home from the food center. It was my mother's cousin Naila who first made contact with the prisoners at Marks House. Still just 16, Naila and her sister Aisha had attended the Canadian Academy, which had both Canadian and American school teachers. It was from her American teachers at the Academy that Naila said she drew sympathy for the American prisoners.

Of my mother's relatives, my Aunt Naila still has one of the most dramatic accents of the group, which is further enhanced by her smoking good looks. I recall growing up seeing Naila, much like Grandma Bacon, dressed in dark colors except that Naila had lips that took to black cigarettes and spoke in an enticing yet un-staged Turkish accent that had the power to draw a young kid far from the holds of an addicting television. She was and still is inviting, articulate, warm, and absolutely enchanting and yet she would never describe herself that way.

Circa 1920-1945. Hussein and Maksura (upper left and right) were brother and sister. Hussein who died of TB at 42 in Kobe was Naila's (bottom left) and Aisha's father, which made my mother (bottom right) a cousin to Naila.

I caught up with Naila just two years ago while she was visiting Seattle and asked her to recall her initial contact with the Americans held at Marks House. Always happy to talk about the past, her face lit up and the details returned clear as a bell and in living color as though it was yesterday. When Naila speaks English, she speaks slowly accentuating and extending syllables. A conversation with her is like dining with someone except what you are enjoying are the new sounds of words rather than the taste of food.

"I leayrned about the preesoners and wahs jahst keeyooreus. I felt so baahd these Ahmerricahns were being held. I started to sneeek food to them baht it was always after darrk, in seeecret. Yeww know, when you're yahhng, you're devil-may-care and you do reesky things."

It was during these visits in October of 1943 that Naila met Woody. Naila insists she just wanted to bring the boys books and help them out and that her interests were merely platonic—at least at first.

"Wooohdy and I did not starrt out as boyfriend-gerlfriend. Baht we ended up that way. And while your mahther and fahther's eenitial meetings in Octohhber were brief because of Mahhksura's concerrns, I was still able to get awaey and continued meeting with Wooohdy."

For Woody who consumed books almost as quickly as he did food, it is hard to say which he favored—the books Naila brought or the food. Needless to say, Naila was fast winning this man's heart over, even if unintentionally.

When I was growing up, my Uncle Woody and Naila lived in Sacramento. He passed away before I ever had a chance—as an adult—to get to know him. He did, however, leave a magnificent diary in which he often wrote of Naila. In one entry he vividly recalled their first encounter.

... *Through Roskowyk, I arranged a date with Naila Altishe, a little Turkish girl who came almost daily to the house next to Marks to get rations for her family. I met her one night October 13, 1943 and then began a romance ... We met on the average of once a week usually by paying camp guards Matsuo and Nakahara 5 yen apiece. After the first few times, Naila began to get Black Market food for me. Eggs, flour, sugar, meat, potatoes, and onions which Jim O'Leary, Bill Gordanie, Bob Hoffstot and myself combined to pay for and consume.*

Up to now Woody and some of the others were actually hopping the fence and sneaking out in the dark of night on occasion. Woody even described venturing to downtown bars and flirting with the local women. The men were also desperate to make black market connections in order to, among other things, supplement their wanting food situation.

In his diary, Woody was very forthcoming. He was candid about having been a bit of a player in his youth, often recalling girlfriends of the past and speculating over lost romances. But as his journal progressed, it became clear that Naila was taking hold of his heart in a deeper and stronger way and that those feelings were starting to rival the best of his fancy memories. He would later write extensively in what can only be described as profound soul-searching as he pondered the future and weighed the two nagging consequences that haunted him. First, if he eventually married Naila, how would it be for her to be separated so far from her family if he were to return to the States with her? And second, if he were to return to the States a married man, would his Catholic family accept Naila? They might have been prisoners of war, but men like Woody and my father were finding these women liberating their hearts and souls and allowing them to speculate with abandon.

Before too long, a third romance would surface as well. Naila's sister Aisha would soon find herself handling books and supplies for Dad's good friend Zane Stickel. It is humorous to recall these young whispering, sneaky Turkish girls with hearts of gold casting their spell on the rough-and-tumble American contractors of Marks House, essentially mowing them over with kindness while inadvertently designating the memories of past American sweethearts to the dust. It is true that my mother and her cousins had the "advantage" of helping to bring the men immediate necessities of life, but that role would soon be tested much more than the women ever expected. It would be a test, however, that would catapult the women farther into the hearts of these American prisoners of war.

PART FIVE:
THE HEART OF WAR

1944: Bitter Winter and Starvation

Conditions worsen for the prisoners as the weather and war darken. Two more men die. Others step up their midnight escapades.

※※※

The winter of '44 was a mixed blessing. Relief arrived as did increased hardships. By December of 1943, Ed still maintained a stiff upper lip in letters home but revealed for the first time the men's needs for basic items.

As it turned out, it was only days after Ed's letter home that his longings for food and clothing finally came true. First, the men received monetary gifts once again from the Pope. Then, on December 23, a truck load of food and clothing from the Red Cross arrived. Each man received one kit. Ed dutifully noted the contents of his kit.

7 packs of cigarettes
3 cans Corned beef
2 bars Swan soap
2 cans of Spam
1 can of KLIM [powdered milk, with the word "milk" spelled backwards]

2 emergency rations of 4 oz chocolate
1 half-pound Borden's American cheese
1 8-oz can of Blue Bird Salmon
2 cans of 4oz. coffee
1 6-oz can Rose mill spread [liver pâté]
1 half-pound box Domino Sugar
4 cans Butter
1 can Peach jam
1 pound box Sugar Drop prunes
1 can opener
1 Army jacket & pants
1 Army overcoat
1 pair Army shoes
1 pair Army underwear
1 pair Army pajamas
2 pair socks
1 Army shirt
1 Army hat
1 pair Army gloves
1 towel
2 handkerchiefs
1 Wool Army sweater
1 Army blanket

Needless to say Ed was ecstatic, not only at the relief of these desperately needed items but from the arrival of mail from the States as well. Many of the men also received packages from home. While Ed did not receive a package, he did get Lucylle's July and August letters. His mother's letters, he would later confess, were the most treasured Christmas gift he ever received.

I just finished a batch of cookies and was wishing I could send some to you. In another letter written on his birthday of July 27, she wrote *I have been thinking of you today as it is your birthday and, of course, I wish you might be here ... As I told you before, I am still home alone as your sister has a position out of town. I sent her a box of cookies last week. I wish I could send some to you as well. This is just a line to let you know we are all well and thinking of you, my dear boy.* Finally, in August, *I was so happy to be able to send you a small package on the ship that is to carry supplies to the internees. The things in the package don't amount to much, only that each one is full of hope and love from your Mother. We are all well and hoping it won't be long before it will all be over. Loads of love, from Mother and All.*

It was a true Christmas for him and the other prisoners. Ed's diary revealed, *All of our thoughts are with our families and even though I am in a prison camp I will never forget this Christmas due to the packages and letters ....*

The mixed blessing to all this was that, as welcomed as the food packages were, they didn't last long. All too soon the men felt the pangs of hunger again. Only a month later, Ed takes to his diary again.

Our rations amount to very little. Need Red Cross food kits badly ... Ones we got at Xmas only lasted 1 week and [the money received] is hardly enough to buy anything now as prices are so high. Weather here is very cold and [the] small amount of food we get makes it that much worse.

Two weeks later Ed's letters and diary magnified his dire straits to the point that even his earlier protocol of hiding his desperation from home no longer held up.

Dearest Mother, Still haven't received your package. We are all hoping for more RCross food as we only rec'd one kit each so far. Hope the State Dept is working on another exchange...will certainly be happy when I get back to the land of Plenty.

Typically, his diary is even more revealing.

Feb 28th No letters. No more RCross food. Mother's package never arrv'd. Weight now at 165. Neck is 14 ½ and waist at 29. Everyone has lost about the same. Everyone is selling what clothing they can for food. One more winter here would be too much. It doesn't look like we're going to get any more RCross food. I think the Japanese Army got most of it already. Things should be getting hot around here in the next few months. If they don't we'll be here forever.

Soon, eating rats was something not unheard of at Marks House. One trick in catching the rodents was to electrocute them. Water pans were rigged between door frames at night. Rats scurrying along would run into the pans and fry. And with prisoners sneaking out at night, many were able to smuggle in, among other things, cooking gear. Men found ways to hide not only the gear but the electrical consumption as well. Clever electricians reversed circuits that foiled meter readings, thereby avoiding suspicion.

Food scarcity was becoming a political issue as well and authorities were trying to stay one step ahead of a potentially embarrassing issue, as my father recalled.

"Once they set up a table in front of us. A cloth was thrown down; then the table was filled with bananas, cherries, apples, and other fruit. Then the press was called in. The idea was to show the press how well the prisoners were being taken care of. Soon as the press left, officials took the fruit and tablecloth away."

By January 1944, in other parts of the world, Hitler's siege of Leningrad ended with nearly one million Soviets dead of starvation while Russia invaded Nazi-occupied Poland. For the Marks House internees, the winter of 1944 was becoming deadly serious as well and beginning to take its toll. At 28 years old, Ed recalled further sobering conditions and the loss of two more inmates.

March 11 Heaviest snow we have had so far.

March 14 Red Cross Rep called at our camp. Second time we have seen one since we have been here. Nat [Martin] Gahley died at the hospital due to lack of care. They have taken one more to the hospital and one is in bed at camp. He should also be at the hospital. Our chances of getting back to America are getting slimmer every day.

March 24 Heavy snow again. Wickman operated on today for gall bladder.

March 30 They say Wickman is doing fine.

April 1 Wickman died last night at 1 a.m. The Japanese called it heart failure but the truth is lack of food .... When a person gets sick and the doctor orders him to the hospital, the head guards will not let them go to the hospital until it's too late. This has been the case of the last three men who died in the last three months.

April 2 Wickman's funeral was today. Two more men from Camp 1 died the same night that Wick died. That makes 7 men in the past few months. There are several sick now. Also there are several of the fellows whose toenails are dropping off.... We are going to have a showdown with the Swiss Consul tomorrow over money, lack of food and all the deaths.

April 11 Carl West and another fella from Camp 1 were operated on this afternoon for appendicitis.

April 27 Didn't think the food could get any worse but it still is. And less every day.

In one of Woody's diary entries, he also appeared furious as he recalled the deaths of some of these same men.

There have been four casualties among the Guam internees. Woodstig and Johnson died in '42 and '43 respectively and Martin Gahley and Harold Wickman, both contractors, died this year [1944] ... Gahley's death was attributed to pneumonia and Wickman's to heart failure. Actually, both men would have been with us today but for criminal negligence on the part of the Japanese Authorities particularly as vested in the so-called attending physician.

The severity of conditions led many of these prisoners into midnight escapades. It was possible to escape Marks house. While Kobe was largely Japanese, it also hosted a diverse international population, as evidenced by Ivet's family, among many others. Still, the risks were obvious. But these were resourceful fellows. Some even ventured out to downtown bars, like Woody had, to flirt with locals. But the main purpose was to make connections to obtain food or money. The black market was becoming serious business for both prisoners and civilians.

During this whole time, Naila was still secretly seeing Woody and, in turn, sharing all this information with Ivet. With hunger for the men becoming critical, my mother's urge to secretly help my father soon outweighed her mother's precautions. Ivet began regularly sneaking off with Naila to help smuggle food to the prisoners. Curiously, my mother and her cousins were not alone in their efforts and, as time would tell, their acts were not going unnoticed.

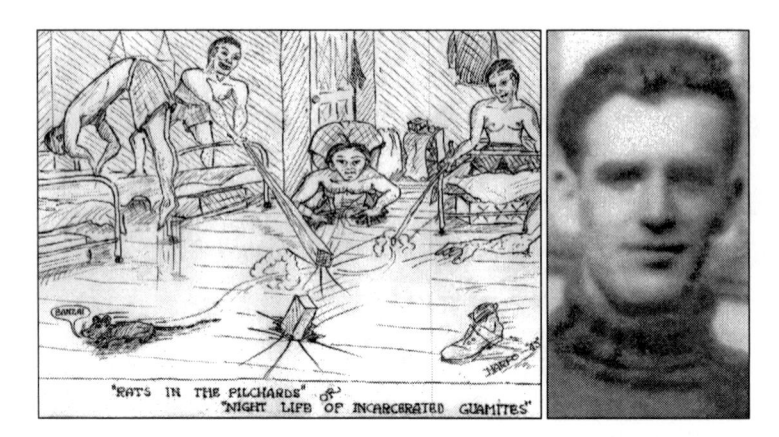

"RATS IN THE PILCHARDS" or
"NIGHT LIFE OF INCARCERATED GUAMITES"

Internee Bob "Harpo" Hoffstot (above right) illustrated the prisoners' frustrations with rodents in 1943. A year later rats were systematically trapped as a food source. Drawing provided by Mike Hoffstot of Washington State. (Below) **Ed's diary.** Typical 1944 entries paint a grim picture.

> Notes
> MAY
>
> May 7th Red Cross Kits arrived at our camp to day but are not being issued yet. Com #3 got theirs May 3rd.
>
> May 13th Issued one kit each to-day. We are going to move by the 20th.
>
> May 26th Moved to another prison camp to day. There are over 160 of us here now. More are to come later. Living conditions are extremely crowded here. In the rooms 11'x15' there are 8 men. Our room is larger but there are 14 in it.
>
> May 31st Our food has been cut down more and even with the kits we just got I'm very hungry.

Futatabi: Ed's Fourth Internment

The men are moved yet again to a mysterious location leaving the women in a panic to find them. Ivet regains contact with Ed but not until after a spellbinding adventure.

It is believed that the Swiss Consul finally demanded that the Japanese authorities move the American prisoners from Marks House farther up the hill. The Swiss argued that the location of Marks House, being closer to downtown, left the prisoners too vulnerable to potential air raids. The Swiss won their argument. On May 26, the men packed what few things they had and were moved to the hills.

According to Woody, prisoners held at Marks House, Butterfield, and the Canadian Academy were all transferred to one location high in the hills of Kobe to the Rinkangaku Building in Futatabi National Park, also known as Hyogo-ken Internment Camp. Rinkangaku, a former summer school for boys, was a good five miles north of Kobe. Sneaking off for food again, while not impossible, was going to be even more difficult now. And although the prisoners were relieved to be moved, some would come to find conditions even more crowded than before with nearly 200 prisoners packed together. The rooms at Futatabi were larger but typically housed 14 men. Woody recalled the new digs.

After 2½ years one becomes quite accustomed to being overcrowded and underfed, and this latest move, rather than being a change for the better, is for the worse in that respect....One advantage is that we can now walk more than 40 feet without running into a 15-foot fence although our walking has been restricted to the lawn in front of our dorms except for the 3 hrs a day when we are permitted to use the school playground which is just too small to play softball on ... not that anyone is getting enough to eat to do any exercise anyway.

1944. Futatabi, Hyogo-ken Internment Camp. The former summer school for boys served as the fourth and last camp where Ed, Woody, and Zane were interned. The men were held at Futatabi for 15 months; they received a pummeling from American air raids at night in the early spring of 1945. Photo by Jack Taylor (*Trapped with the Enemy*).

Transferring that many men was no doubt risky business for the Japanese. A pattern of weakening prisoners prior to a move seems to have been common practice. By the time the men entered Futatabi, they were wasted, as both Woody and Ed recalled.

So far we have had nothing to eat but soggy bread which we have had to haul up a 10% grade for about 5 miles daily, boiled cabbage and a pitifully meager supply of dirty rice, wrote Woody.

Even with the kits we got last month our food has been cut further and I am very hungry, my father told his diary.

While the men settled in, the girls were in an absolute panic. They had no idea there were plans to move the prisoners. Suddenly the men were gone. The ordeal of trying to find the men and finally hooking up with them again was a hair-raising story my mother often told.

"We didn't know what happened, where they took them or anything. Then one day Naila met a Chinese cook who used to work at Marks House. Finally, through him she found out they had moved the men to Futatabi. Naila sent a note through this Chinese cook and regained communications with the boys.

"One day Naila, her sister Aisha, and I decided to go up the mountain to Futatabi. The cook had gotten a note back from the men describing a meeting place. To get out of the house, I was trying to think of a good excuse in case it took us a long time to get back. I told Mother I was going to the Club.

"The three of us were to meet at the bottom of the hill so we could go up together. I showed up first. I waited and waited. An hour went by and the girls still didn't show. I figured they'd left without me so I started up the hill, hesitated a little, but then thought I'd meet them there. I knew where the meeting place was so I started to climb. At some point I had to go through a Japanese Army camp. I got through alright. The meeting place was five or six miles up the hill. I was so hot and I remember I was dressed in white. White skirt and white blouse. I didn't want to get all wet and perspired so I took off my blouse. I knew nobody used this path. But as I was taking my blouse off, there was an air raid siren that started whistling. Then I heard someone coming, running at fast speed. I ducked. He was running so fast he didn't see me. He was a soldier. I didn't know where he was coming from but my heart was beating through my chest I was so scared and so glad he didn't see me. Crouched down, holding my blouse, I stopped for a minute to catch my breath.

"I started up the hill again. As I was getting close to the meeting place, I heard another noise behind me so I ducked again. My heart was pounding so hard. I thought the soldier I'd passed was coming back. I didn't know what to do. All of a sudden the figure appeared. It was my brother Sam! I didn't know what to make of it. I asked him what he was doing. He told me he'd been spying on me and knew I was going up to see the boys. I thought he was going to be so mad. Instead he looked at me confused and said, 'Why didn't you let me help you?' He explained that he was doing black marketing himself and he was able to get anything, showing me all kinds of canned goods he had with him. I became so relieved and happy to see him."

My Uncle Sam was another very generous soul. Jet black hair, chiseled jaw line, slender build, and a hearty laugh that used all the muscles and expression his handsome face had to offer. My mother said when they were younger, Sam was the kind of guy who, at a dance, would notice the one girl who was being ignored—and ask *her* to dance. He was much more loquacious than his siblings, and throughout his life he remained one of my mother's best friends, calling her endlessly to come visit him during his retirement years. This recollection of how he helped my mother smuggle food never surprised me.

"When we got to the meeting place, nobody was there," my mother continued. "I didn't know what to do. Pretty soon the three boys [Ed, Woody, and Zane] came out of the bushes relieved to finally see us. When they began asking where the others were, I told them what happened. Before too long, Aisha and Naila showed up happy to see the boys and then naturally wondering what in the world Sam was doing there. I told them the whole story about climbing up there and how he had surprised me.

"We were all amused and relieved and everything turned out fine. We had a good time and now we had a place to visit. Coming back home at one point, we started running down the hill. Once I started running down, it was so hard to stop. I tried grabbing bushes, tripped, and went rolling down just barely missing a cliff. In the process I sprained my ankle. When I got home, I had to tell Mother I tripped on the subway on the way home from the Club."

Angel of Mercy: Ivet Takes Action

BOTH ED AND WOODY BECOME VERY ILL. HEARING THE NEWS, IVET SHIFTS COURSE AND DETERMINES TO SAVE HER MAN.

Reuniting with each other was clearly the one and only bright spot for Ed and Ivet during the early summer of 1944. By then, the D-Day landing of Allied forces in Normandy had proved successful, and the U.S. remained heavily engaged in Europe as well as making advances in the Philippines, Guam, and Saipan. Roosevelt met with MacArthur in Hawaii at about this time, and B-29 raids had begun on Japan. For my father, prison life was deteriorating further. He continued to receive mail from home six and seven months later. Food was becoming scarcer, and he was chronically hungry. By July, Ed, Woody, and others were becoming very ill. Woody's diary took note.

July 14 Edmonds and Manley went to the hospital yesterday. Bacon had some heart trouble last night and I am feeling as weak as I ever have been.

July 16 Still in bed. Weaker'n hell ... jaundice condition is settling in. Missed mass this morning.

July 19 Bacon has come down with the same [jaundice] ailment.

Aug 3 Food scarcer and more poorly prepared ....No water for anything from 4:00 o'clock on.

Aug 5 On July 18th I came down with a fever which lasted 8 days turning into Yellow Jaundice. My eyes and body are still very yellow. Getting along pretty good until last night and had a relapse. All my bones ache badly and pain in my liver. Weigh less than 150 lbs, waist 27 inches. The doctor refuses to come up unless he can get 500 yen. There have been 8 cases of this. Mine has lasted the longest. Been taking 20cc of calcium and metabolism shots intravenously daily. The camp is getting worse off every day. We have been out of water for the past 2 months, only enough for drinking and it has to be boiled due to dead rats in the well.

Aug 29 Tipped the scales at 149 lbs fully dressed. ... Dutch Haller, from Guam, is dying in his bed and we can't even get him to a hospital.

Sept 11 Got permission tonight to move Bacon to sick bay. Poor kid is a lot sicker than he knows. Hope we can build him up again.

Of course this is two days before Ed wrote his sister saying *health okay, don't worry*. And while Woody recovered enough to sneak out for supplies and a *stolen hour with [his] honey*, his health plummeted once again.

Sept 22 Came back from Sick Bay last night. Have been in and out of there since Sept 7 with malnutrition, fever, night sweats, sore teeth, swollen gums, raw tongue and white spots on my throat.

During this time Ed's diary entries slowed and his handwriting is visibly smaller. Woody's entries, on the other hand, tended to pick up with his discussions of camp and world politics, increasing air raid sirens, and the steady stream of books he devoured. Finally, another fatality occurred. On October 13, Woody's diary mourned the death of Dutch Haller noting *He weighed less than 90 pounds.*

At one point in the summer Ed was at his lowest, weighing even less than Woody. At 137 pounds Ed had lost nearly 70 pounds. This was also a time when Woody engaged in a great deal of soul searching in his diary. Woody began seriously considering the consequences of marrying Naila, which would mean taking her far away from her family. Camp politics was, at times, driving him nuts with its backbiting and petty arguments.

And it was a time when his relationship with Ed solidified. Perhaps it was the shared interest they had in related girlfriends, his compassion for Ed during a serious illness paired with the frustrating camp politics that all led Woody to conclude at one point, *I quite realize now ... the best friends I have are right here with me and, in the main, the few of them that are really friends ... will be my closest associates for some time in the States ... Jim [Thomas], Bacon, Harpo, Bill, Leon—there are only a few.*

Meanwhile, Ivet was happy just to have regained communication with Ed although with the escalating war, her mother was beginning to keep an even greater protective eye on her, requiring Ivet to come up with better excuses for going here and there. If Ivet was having a hard time getting out, she found she could at least help Naila with black market exchanges.

"In Naila's family, there were six children and only a mother to support them. Naila's mother used to be a seamstress. They couldn't afford black market and it was very hard to find those things unless you had contacts. Baba had a lot of contacts with his business. Soon we became pretty well supplied with food. I used to go out to the farm houses. You couldn't buy food but could exchange things like clothes or shoes for food. After I'd get food, on the way home I used to hide some of it and give it to Naila to smuggle to the camp."

Soon, Naila got word to Ivet about Ed's failing health—news that fostered Naila's ulterior motives. "Woody eventually told me he intended to marry me. My reaction was no way, I was too young. But as time went on, I began to care for him. I admit, I began to think that if I could keep others involved such as Ivet and Aisha, that maybe I could marry this guy. Maksura was later very mad at me for involving the others."

Certainly, Naila knew all too well that Ivet, born with an inoperable Florence Nightingale streak in her, would be unable to resist the challenge, the duty, the irrepressible urge within her to get food to that suffering man she had, by now, grown to love.

There was something about Ivet that was true about her then and always. Donned in poise and civility, Ivet shared all the qualities of the fictional June Cleaver television character: meek and mild, willing to please, nurture, and serve forever and ever. However, the difference with

Ivet was that if anything ever threatened her loved ones, she could morph into mother-bear mode leaving only two things certain. One, no one dared stand in her way. And two, nothing changed her mind. This morphing was a once-in-a-while event. But when it did happen, it was the kind of thing that left eyes and mouths wide open. One did not mess with her under those conditions. Telling Ivet that Ed was suffering was all it took to put her into action.

Soon enough Ivet hatched a plan to find a place to pitch a tent halfway up the hill to make the trip to Futatabi easier. A place far enough away to avoid suspicion and one that offered a perfect alibi. What better place than her sister Farida's cottage nestled farther up the hill from Ivet's home? It was a good rest stop between the girls' neighborhood and Futatabi and where Ivet could "visit" her sister. Farida later recalled what seemed an innocent harbinger.

"During the war we lived up the hill from Aba and Baba's in a cottage my husband Shy had built for us. At some point I noticed the girls had pitched a tent just below the cottage and started almost living there. I thought they were doing this to avoid the air raids. I was too busy with the kids and my in-laws, selling our rations and bartering for soap to think much of their tent. It wasn't until later that I found out about their schemes."

However, back home Rashid wasn't too busy not to notice his sneaky little sister.

"The girls were always taking something from the house. I used to wonder what was going on but I never asked questions. Pop [Safa] would go out to the country to buy potatoes and rice from the farmers. He would bring this back and I would see him hide it. Then I would see Ivet take a little and then be gone from the house for a long time. I had suspicions the girls were meeting the Americans, but I didn't say anything because I myself had earlier snuck down to Marks House to exchange black market items. I used to ride by on my bike and toss things over the fence."

Ivet's plans soon picked up pace. With her perfect alibi along with her "farm subsidies," Ivet also helped herself to both Sam's and Baba's hefty black market stashes in their backyard. Now she could "visit" Farida while trotting back and forth from tent to camp—all to save her man.

It was precisely the kind of mission that transformed this otherwise gentle, wistful creature into a driven, fearless, risk-taking, get-out-of-my-way angel of mercy. This transformation was an almost humorous part of my mother that she exhibited throughout her life. Whether it was racing up the hills of Kobe strictly against her mother's wishes or pushing a nurse out of the way driving my father in a wheelchair through a Burlingame emergency room or straining her aged back to lift him from a fall later in life, I am not sure I have ever witnessed another person's unmitigated relentlessness to insure the survival of another person's life than my mother's determination for my father's life. It is, therefore, quite easy to picture a young Ivet, swimming champion no less, taking on the hills of Futatabi weighed down with stolen rations yet pure of heart and hopefully absolving her sins of theft in the saving of at least one skinny life in the midst of a group of starving men in one Hyogo-ken Internment Camp in the hills of Japan.

The Stickel-Bacon-Woodruff Company

The men's health improves and so does their resolve. Smuggling becomes a serious business—along with consequences.

❧❧❧

By the fall of 1944, Ed's health was returning and his letters were those of a man truly yearning for home. He repeatedly thanked his family for the letters from the year before that he'd received. He would plead for them to send more photos and save him a piece of pie. Muse over future jobs in the States. Inquire of his friends back home. Still insist his health was fine. And while he'd met a wonderful gal, he also yearned for the home he'd left. For the *land of plenty.* To see *the Golden Gate in 48* and some of that *good ole Frisco fog.*

With his letters being censored, it would have been foolish for Ed to have mentioned to his family all the help Ivet was doing for him. But certainly, the nightingale's work was paying off as were the Red Cross kits, newly ordered Congressional stipends, and a formidable black market ring at camp. Ed was not only writing again but also by November he was up to 170 pounds. And as his health slowly returned in that fall, he found a place in the kitchen. Both Ed and Bob Hoffstot, also known as "Harpo," were mentioned at least twice in Woody's diary *turning out rare delicacies and chocolate cakes.* Ed's sweet tooth, denied for so long, was making a comeback.

As they approached their fourth year of captivity, the guys got down to business. They were not going to endure this next winter like they had the previous ones. Call it American ingenuity in captivity, human survival instinct, rising determination, or the combination of all those with, of course, the help of their Turkish sweethearts. In December Woody wrote, *If we were totally dependent on Mess Hall food for our sustenance, we'd be ready for the undertaker by now.* Even with the Red Cross kits, they knew they had to supplement themselves.

Ed's journal included many lists such as this one documenting black market exchange rates in Kobe during the winter of 1944.

Woody's health was returning as well and his leadership skills were re-emerging both in camp and in the black market. In Futatabi, Woody lost his earlier paranoia of the "prying eyes" of camp guards. Here he began another diary and we learn more about camp politics at this time. He got elected as one of the camp leaders. He met with authorities to negotiate Red Cross supplies and distribution. With nearly 200 prisoners, this became a daunting task, tapping into those organizational skills Woody wielded as a supervisor in Guam. Thus, order was emerging within the camp and Woody was very much responsible for it.

Ed as well was trying to organize his life, what there was of it. Whether out of boredom or in an effort to remain productive, his journal not only included diary entries and letters but lists of goods, black market price sheets, coded messages, yearly price comparisons, gift ledgers, calendar diagrams, and a cash account record.

For the prisoners, camp order took on two forms. First, the open order of the camp guards, protocol, rules, official camp leaders, and their relations with authorities. Second, the secret order of the internees' underground wheeling and dealings, their poker games, and their growing outside connections. By now Woody managed to sneak off and meet Naila for black market exchanges about once a week. Soon enough he had others joining him in these late-night escapades, and by now many of the men were able to trade.

The U.S. Congress had ordered PNAB to honor the contracts with their now detained civilian work force. Consequently, many of the men started receiving small monthly stipends from the State Department as well as the gifts from the Red Cross and the Swiss Consul. Still, according to Ed, what one would call their income only amounted to about $20 a month, and many men had been gambling their stipends and Red Cross supplies away at camp. It was not unusual for the guys to be winning and losing 100-200 yen a night in a poker game—an amount nearly comparable to a month's salary back in the U.S. Part of the reason many were drawn to gambling was inflation. Things were getting too expensive to buy and prices continued to skyrocket. According to Ed, in January of 1944 sugar was 15 yen per pound. By December it shot up to 100 yen a pound with a black market exchange rate of 2.5 yen to the dollar. Save or gamble? Both were risky.

Taking a cue from the adage that there is strength in numbers, my father and others joined forces to create what Woody coined the "Stickel-Bacon-Woodruff Company." Using collective funds, Red Cross goods, and rendezvous efforts of these men, including Harpo, with Naila, Ivet, and

Aisha, they started a rather high-stakes black market exchange in which the quantities of goods became significant.

By mid-December Woody reported that *Bacon, Stickel, and myself brought back 75 pounds of flour and 9 pounds of spuds.* In black market terms, that was about 2,000 yen, or 6 months' worth of a teacher's income back home. It is unclear exactly how long the Company lasted. A safe guess is eight to ten weeks with a core of about a half dozen men running as night riders.

The Company had two simple goals in mind: food and survival. What is clear is that they had quite a run with it, at least for a time.

Unfortunately, as the first of the year approached, Woody worried. *We're into [fellow internee] Leo about 2,000 yen and financing is becoming difficult.* Woody estimated that the company's inventory was at 5,000 yen by then and was going to have to get them through the winter and possibly the war while at the same time he sensed the company was developing stretch marks.

The clandestine capers took on significant outcomes, all of which came at a cost. The risks involved, the money gambled, the approaching winter, the uncertainty of hunger amid growing air raids—all added a degree of stress that began to fray relationships. Not only was it maddening to try to keep up with soaring prices but by December it was also beginning to snow. The snow made for an even more difficult trek up and down the hills of Kobe and sneaking out meant leaving a trail of midnight footprints as well.

Their other lifeline of Red Cross supplies was also becoming tenuous. There was no way to be certain that the increasing air raids were going to meticulously target everything but Red Cross supply lines heading up the heavily wooded mountain side. In fact, the sounds of air raid sirens were beginning to fill the air longer and more often along with the quarrels of Woody and Zane over company logistics while the clatter of at least one manual typewriter simultaneously ticked away as Harpo put to print his official letter of resignation from the company.

This was the essence of the company in the early winter of 1944 at Futatabi: high yields with high stress. A little bit like trying to enjoy caviar—on the Titanic. The company was rocky but still in business. Finally, it was the incessant air raids that reminded everyone how increasingly vulnerable supply lines were becoming. Ed's December entry captures some of the tension.

Dec. 18th Planes came over Osaka this morning and again this afternoon over Kobe. Altho the guards ran us all in the Mess Hall we still saw several B29 at approximately 20,000 feet. They leave quite a streak of smoke. The Japanese planes couldn't get halfway to them. The raid lasted from 1-3 pm. We are hoping the Red Cross supplies get up to the camp before they're blown all over Japan.

Just days before Christmas of 1944, Ed noted two more air raids lasting up to three hours each. Then, what would seem a last-meal gesture on the part of the Japanese, Ed noted an unusual feast.

Christmas, and tonight they gave us the largest meal we've had: salted herring, roast beef, fish, eggs and apple pie.

Unfortunately, as the prisoners had gone from feast to famine so often throughout their internment, one month later, Woody conceded the Bacon-Stickel-Woodruff company was *on the rocks*.

> After considerable contemplation I have decided I want to with-draw from our combine. I realize that you, Woody, have been my meal ticket for quite a while and I appreciate it very much. On the other hand I, also put in quite a number of hours toward you well-being and I feel that we are about "even Steven" but that is for you, Bake and Stick to decide.
>   My reasons: I want to be free from <u>all</u> responsibility. I don't want any ties what-so-ever with any individual. I want to strickly "<u>Lone Wolf it</u>" in everything. I feel that this is essential to my mental well-being.
>   For my share of the remaining Red Cross food of the company, I will be satisfied with one of the cans of meat. And an even split between you and I, Woody. As for the other food and b.m.stuff I leave entirely up to you. As you have have handled the finace. I have no idea where I stand. Any settlement you make will be entirely satisfactory to me. The things such as shoe polish, butter etc. that we are now using together may remain the same untill finished. Such things as were bought together, rope, bucket, tea pot, etc., may remain the same.
>   I would like to use the stove once in a while and I would appreciate it very much if you ever have any surplus food and would sell it to me. I am <u>not</u> mad at any of you, singularly or collectively. I hope we remain as good friends as we have been.
>   My mind is made up in this matter. Any argument or discussion is only a waste of your time and mine. So please let this go no further I have put this in writing so I could have my complete say with out any heated discussion. Also so you, Woody, can show Bake and Stick.
>
>   Harp.

Bob "Harpo" Hoffstot sends Woody an amicable letter of resignation from the Stickel-Bacon-Woodruff Company. Harpo decided to "lone wolf it," regarding securing his own supplies as winter approached.

St. Patrick's Day Bombing

Japan suffers her heaviest bombings during 1945. A March 17 attack was particularly gruesome for the internees high in the Futatabi hills.

***

By early 1945, Paris, Brussels, and Auschwitz had all been liberated and the Soviet Union, United States, and Britain were convening the Yalta Conference to discuss post-war Europe. As for American forces, they were moving fast and furious in the South Pacific. They had landed in the Philippines, captured Iwo Jima, and were on the way to Okinawa. Japan herself would face heavy fire power as well. For the next nine months, American forces conducted air campaigns on all the major cities of Japan, not the least of which was Kobe.

Both Ed and Ivet were now consumed with having to master the black market in order to survive. Even civilian clothing rations were cut in half by this time.[16] Now they would have to endure air raids on top of this, sometimes with heart-wrenching consequences.

---

[16] *The Library of Congress World War II Companion.* (2007). New York: Simon & Schuster, 881.

As Ed faced another difficult winter month in the low 20°s, he gave no hint of air raids, bombings, or camp deaths in letters home. Instead, he simply told his family, *things have changed here a lot.* He did offer some tongue-in-cheek advice for his sister. *Glad to see Marj is traveling, but tell her to keep it within the States. Island trips don't work out so well.*

The more the air raids increased, the more often Ed's letters suggested a veiled optimism ... *things are getting better over here ... there is a lot to say but very little I can write ... I think I'll be home for Christmas this year.* As usual, Ed's diary was more revealing, such as the entry of January 19th.

Today they dropped heavy bombs here in Kobe for the first time. They shook hell out of the buildings. Two raids last night. Four raids in the last 48 hours. Hardly a day or night goes by without one now. Today was a good one and quite a sight to see.

At least the men were surviving. There was a feeling of being a little better prepared this year with enough food for a couple of months. The men were even allowed to burn wood in their stoves to keep warm—a new comfort, according to Woody. One pictures Woody stoking the flames before reclining to write, with similar vividness, of the recent raid, which included the neighboring town.

Eighty planes hit this area on the 19th, quite a sight. Reports are that Akashi was severely damaged and one can well believe it as the shock of bombs dropping there shook the buildings here, some 10-odd miles away.

At first, the Company decided no more trips due to the increased air raids. But "fools rush in where wise men never go," and the fellows continued their secret meetings with the girls, exchanging goods and stealing kisses amidst the ubiquitous air raid sirens. Once they returned to find more fatalities at camp. In mid-January, two internees, Kopp and Pourbaix, both succumbed to heart failure. *Nakasaka, one of the good guards,* Ed wrote, *also died unexpectedly at camp the same week.*

February and March were even worse for air raids. Alerts became so frequent that Ed created a daily air raid chart, distinguishing whether the raids hit morning, noon, or night. Ed remembered there were three raids on February 4 in which he described Kobe as a city *ablaze of flames.*

Woody's diary concurred, adding that the B-29s spent two hours that day dropping incendiaries and *30 hours later the city was still burning.*

It was at this point that the Company took stock again of what it had. This time the men finally determined it was too dangerous to make any more midnight runs. With the last of their Red Cross kits issued and 18° weather, they were just going to have to hunker down and hope the food held out until the weather warmed.

Meanwhile, just miles below Futatabi, Ivet's brother Rashid was getting a closer view of the raids pummeling the city. Sitting on a rooftop, mesmerized by the sights and sounds down below, he could almost view this as entertainment because he was always a safe distance away—until one time in particular.

"I used to have a front row seat. Just like Hillside Drive in Burlingame sits above the Bay Area, our home sat in the hills above the ports of Kobe. During the raids I used to go up on our roof to watch. It was out of this world. The anti-aircraft fire and all. I wasn't scared. I felt safe watching from the roof, at least in the beginning. Later, I remember a 5-pound anti-personnel bomb landed close by sending off shrapnel. It hit homes a half a block away from us and even killed some people in the neighborhood. At that time, though, I still didn't feel like I was going to get hit. Of course things soon changed.

"Later, as these air raids increased, the women were told to go up to the hills for protection. I always stayed behind with Pop. Except once. It was during a 12-hour raid. Port bombs started coming closer to the house and I thought I was going to have to run for the hills myself. I don't remember telling Dad I was going. Sam and the others were at our country cabin in Arima.

"I headed up about 100 yards into the forest above our home. There were jelly bombs all over the place. The jelly would ignite with a ball of fire whatever it stuck to, like rubber igniting. The whole area was inflamed. There was no way you could stop it. I was all by myself for hours and this time I was really scared. Finally, when I heard the all-clear sirens, I went back home. When I arrived, Pop was outside offering street people water. People were walking around dazed. 'Where have you been? You should have been here,' he scolded me. I put my things down and started helping him."

Ed's Air Raid and Supply Log charts the good, the bad, and the ugly of the spring of 1945 at the Futatabi prison camp.

This same air raid was one that both Ivet and Sam remembered as well. They were coming home from Arima and passed through a downtown rail station destroyed by bombings. They recalled bodies hanging from car windows and train cars derailed, blackened, and still smoking from ruin. It then became a race to get home to make sure Baba and Rashid had escaped the intensity of the air raid. Fortunately they had, although Sam learned a few days later that many of his friends who lived in town had been killed in the raid.

For the men at Futatabi, however, nothing quite compared to the March 17 air raid, the St Patrick's Day Bombing, as Ed and Woody called it. By March, despite their earlier reservations about sneaking out, the men were still making restless and admittedly foolish runs to town.

One of the things they were able to grab downtown was newspapers. Woody wrote that *the Japanese were becoming increasingly worried about the impending landing on the mainland.* The Japanese concerns were well founded. While American forces hadn't yet landed in Japan, in the early morning hours of March 17, more than 300 B-29s penetrated Kobe air space. It was another day etched graphically in both Ed's and Woody's diaries.

At about 2 a.m. the men were awakened by an emergency air raid alert and the sounds of swarming American aircraft. According to Woody, the B-29s worked in teams of three, dropping flares and incendiary bombs at low altitude, and both Japanese and American fighter planes soon became visible in Japanese searchlights. The raid lasted three hours, after which both Kobe and Akashi cooked in flames, lighting even the distant skies of Futatabi.

By 5 a.m. the raid was coming to an end. According to Woody, the men, shaken and dazed, tried to settle in as best they could when suddenly at 6,000 feet a Japanese pilot rammed a B-29, ripping the American fighter plane in half directly above camp. As quickly as the men ran out to see what was going on, they turned again for cover as the tail section came whistling through the red sky, landing about 400 feet from camp while the other half of the plane sent down a metal hail-storm with parts taking out the laundry room and the cook's shack in a ball of fire.

Some men were said to be shouting and pointing with gruesome speculation. *Two parachutes could be seen descending and some of the fellows claim to have seen other bodies fall without their 'chutes having opened,* Woody wrote.

As daylight increased, the discoveries were shocking. First, men began hauling machine parts in from all directions of the camp including four huge motors, which had landed just outside the building. Then a body was found, only 50 feet from Woody's room. The flyer's parachute was unopened, still strapped to his back. Woody could not make out whether the man's name was Bouland or Boulard.

Zane later ventured further into the hills. He was first to discover the tail section with *five horribly mutilated bodies,* Woody wrote. At noon, a Japanese child was said to have come trotting into the camp calling for the guards to follow him. He and the guards returned a half hour later with one of the B-29 crew members caked in blood, with a cut over his eye. Described as an otherwise good-looking, well-built kid about 22, by the name of Nelson, the pilot was escorted incommunicado until officials arrived and took him away. A second American crew member was found alive below camp, with a broken leg. His name was believed to have been August, a 22-year-old from upstate New York, who was discovered sitting by the wreckage with a liter of morphine wrapped around him. Days later the Japanese would discover a seventh body, also strapped to his chair, in the woods just over the hill from camp.

After two weeks the prisoners were allowed to revisit the wreckages to bury the dead. Both Ed and Woody made efforts to glean as much information from the crash site, copying down names and numbers. According to Ed, the wreckage was of the 315th Bombing Wing. They also found what appeared to be the dog tags of at least two of the five airmen, John T. Berry 16,141602 T42-43A and Dave W. Holley 17,097498 T43-44O. Woody described the first airman as James T. Berry and added a third name, that of R. E. Copeland. Woody transcribed the wreckage as *plane No. 629 attached to the 29th squadron, 373rd bombing wing.*

In all, 9 airmen were accounted for with only 2 surviving the crash, a horrific ending to the ravaging St Patrick's Day bombing, which, at Futatabi, shook the core of both the Japanese and Americans there. It is estimated that half of Tokyo, Kobe, and Yokohama was destroyed by the March bombings.[17] As for Kobe, she was hit hard. Nearly 9,000 people were believed killed and over 600,000 homes destroyed. It was said Kobe burned for a week. "An appalling sight," according to Max, one of Woody's midnight runners.

---

[17] *The Library of Congress World War II Companion.* (2007). NY: Simon & Schuster, 888.

1945. Kobe. *Showa History of 100 Million People: Occupation of Japan Vol.2.* Published by Mainichi Newspaper Company.

Naila and Woody Caught

As the war escalates, security tightens. Both Woody and Naila discover this the hard way.

⁂

As the air raids on Kobe increased, not surprisingly, security tightened with the prisoners. And while the consensus of the men was that being caught going to town could very well mean being shot, it still didn't stop them from venturing. Nor did it stop Naila. Only two weeks after the St. Patrick's Day raid, Woody made another horrifying discovery.

Received word that Naila had been picked up by the Kencho, held for 9 hours, slapped around some, threatened and questioned until she finally told them about meeting me and carrying notes back and forth. Then was released with instructions to tell her family that she was erroneously suspected and not to mention anything about the connection up here.

Naila remembered her day in jail quite well and blamed everything on, of all things, a jealous tattletale.

"A local girl named Maria was the daughter of a British subject also held at Futatabi. She would visit her dad at the camp. At some point, she found out about Woody and me and, out of jealousy, tattle-taled to guards about us. The authorities came to my house and told my mother they wanted to talk to me. They took me downtown to Headquarters and interrogated me all day. Japan was beginning to lose the war by this time and they wanted to know if I was spying. Was I providing short-wave radios to the prisoners? I insisted over and over that all I did was give the prisoners food and pots and pans, which I had taken from my mother. This went on for hours and I was quite frightened. Finally they let me go at the end of the day."

Not taking any cues from this, Woody continued to venture downtown himself for more food runs as power had been out at camp for days. Food was scarce again. Woody was only eating twice a day. He was also desperate to find out more, if anything, about Naila. Then, just days after Naila's interrogation, Woody and Max were caught halfway down the hill on their way to town.

According to Woody, the two were brought back to camp for a *teeth sucking lecture* from the guards. The guards were especially mad at Woody, who was the assistant camp leader at the time. For some reason, Woody concocted a story about meeting contacts at the outskirts of town. What he failed to expect was that the authorities would be curious to meet these people. Woody and Max were thus escorted downtown to the fictitious meeting place. Woody recalled what happened next.

... Finally, after waiting in the rain for an hour for our 'phonies' to show up, they took us to the Kencho and thence to the Kikusuibashi Police Station where we were booked and tossed into a 8' x 5' cell—as filthy a hole I ever have or hope to see.

Needless to say, both Naila and Woody were very lucky. Apparently, at this point in the war, authorities were more concerned if folks were passing sensitive information than if they were merely scrambling for food. Since both managed to convince authorities of the latter, they were eventually let off the hook.

As crazy as it may seem, and despite Woody having been caught, sitting back and behaving themselves was still not an option to some of the men. Power was out. Supplies were low. Prices were through the roof (sugar still at 100 yen a pound). For Ed, it had seemed an eternity since he'd last seen the Red Cross. Hunger had become an issue again.

Woody noted that with security tightened the men had to get even more creative. He recalled that in early May, when a surprise roll-call caught two men missing, others snuck out to whisk the two back to camp. Just before arriving at camp, the retrievers handed the two missing men a sack of B-29 parts and smeared their faces with grease. The ruse worked. The two men strolled back into camp. And while their greasy faces were soon greeted by scolding guards—who believed the two left without permission to visit the crash site—it was a far cry to what would have been another escorted trip downtown.

By the end of May, relief came in the form of more Red Cross supply kits. This time men were given two boxes each. These kits were a god-send for the men. Unfortunately, and once again, the boxes only lasted 10 days. The men would need more outside help.

Air Raids and a Silver Ring

Ivet recalls the horrors of her neighborhood bombings and more than one near-fatal incident, while at camp Ed ponders a crash site and crafts a token of love.

※※※

With the war in Europe nearing its end, the South Pacific was heating up. Mussolini had been executed, German troops had surrendered in Italy, and Hitler had committed suicide. Meanwhile, American forces had liberated Manila and landed on Okinawa.

It was about this time Woody heard radio news that a barrage of B-29s and P-51s had raided Yokohama for two hours. But the men took little notice of this. Perhaps it was becoming commonplace. The weather was warming. The men were even playing baseball with the guards, and at least three of the other prisoners were said to be off in the woods, *picnicking with g-gals*. It was the proverbial calm before the storm.

Finally, the storm hit once again. On June 5, more than 400 American B-29s forged a battalion into what was said to be Kobe's largest raid. This time Ivet's neighborhood was hit hard.

"The day of the biggest air raid, there were hundreds of planes. We could see them from our veranda. The whole sky was moving. I remember

Baba calling to all of us to get out of the house. We all took a few of our needed things, which we had prepared for in case of this kind of raid. Dad would never go. He used to say that someone had to stay to protect the home, not just from the raid but from looters as well. I used to cry and beg him to come but he insisted on staying. Crying and angry, I finally took to the hills with the others. I remember a mass of people running through our streets to get to shelters. There were others looting homes as well. There were many days like this. We always came home safe but many areas below us would be destroyed. Ships, factories, buildings—all blown up.

A 17-year-old Shamil (my Uncle Sam) among the ruins of the bombed-out Canadian Academy, a school he once attended.

"But this raid in June was so big. I especially remember the shower of incendiary bombs. Whatever they hit would ignite in fire. Even water on the ground would evaporate instantly. This is what destroyed the city. This was the scariest raid.

"After about two hours of bombing, when the planes finally left, everybody started leaving the shelter. On the way home we came across many people with burns over their bodies, screaming for help.

"I remember crying and running through the flames of houses. We thought sure our house was gone and Dad too. I was running and crying in the mass of humans and flames. We finally saw Baba fighting the fire. We ran to him, so glad to see him. Then we started to help him save our house. The whole city burned all day. What a sight it was—very scary!"

During this raid Farida was in Kobe trying to get home. She recalled that the downtown had beautiful fountains in the shopping areas but on this day, the raids etched an unforgettable horror as she witnessed scores of people rushing into the fountains to escape the incendiary bombs only to be boiled alive in front of her as the fountains themselves became targets.

By the time it was over, it was said that more than four square miles of the city was destroyed.[18] Had the prisoners not been moved earlier, this raid would have likely killed my father and many others as Marks House was turned to rubble. The Sidline house next door was also completely destroyed although the Sidlines miraculously survived. Still, no doubt some of the prisoners were thinking they hadn't been moved far enough up the hill, as Futatabi was not spared either. It was one of the few entries in Ed's journal that stopped mid-sentence.

June 5th Largest mass raid on Kobe. Our hospital was burned up today as well as all our Red Cross supplies. The—

According to Ivet, the raids did not stop there. They seemed to be endless during the summer of 1945. Sam was nearly killed twice. She was nearly killed once herself as she tried to make her way up to see Ed.

"These raids went on every day on and off for weeks until they destroyed all the factories and war supply areas. I remember during one of these raids as we were running up to the shelter, a plane flew down and machine-gunned us, just missing Sam. He was nearly killed. Another time he'd gotten hit with a jelly bomb while he was running away with his clothes catching on fire. I was so scared.

"On another occasion I was pinned down in a gutter. I had snuck out and was trying to get up to see Ed. I couldn't quite make it all the way up the hill. Halfway there, another air raid began. You could hear the whistling of the bombs before they landed. I heard that whistling. This time it was much closer. I quickly ducked for cover. Suddenly I felt the impact of the bomb and debris that came showering down on top of me. I was

---

[18] http://www.nationmaster.com/encylcopedia/Bombing-of-Kobe-in-World-War-II.

frozen. I didn't move until it was all over. I thought for sure I was going to be killed. After that experience, I was the first to run to the hills when the raids started."

By August of 1945, some 6,000 tons of bombs had been dropped on cities throughout Japan.[19]

Meanwhile, back at camp, the much earlier St Patrick's Day air raid was still on the men's minds. The crash site was often visited. One day Ed went to the site alone. In the rubble he stumbled upon a coin. It was a 1939 American dime with the word *Liberty* scrolled across the upper rim. The coin had apparently fallen out of one of the pilots' pockets. As he held the coin, the crash site suddenly took on a very personal feel. He began thinking of the young airman. When did he get the coin? What would he have bought with it and what would he have done with his life? He was just one of thousands who had given his life in this thicket of war but whose life had value for somebody somewhere much like this little coin shining in the dense woods of Futatabi.

As he pondered the ring, it made him think of Ivet as well and all she had been doing for him. It was one thing for her to have stopped by the Marks House and smuggled a few treats to him. It was, after all, on the way to pick up the family rations. But now she was trekking up and down a war-ravaged hillside for him with food and dodging who knows what. She didn't *have* to do that. Certainly Arlene wouldn't have gone that far. He was seeing Ivet in a new light. No one had ever sacrificed that much, just for him. He was used to being self-reliant and was very good at it, but now he was nearly skin and bones. Besides his romantic affections for her, he truly *needed* Ivet. In his eyes she was not only gorgeous and engaging, she was becoming more importantly genuine. He was overwhelmed with gratitude and falling deeply in love.

Ed brought the coin back to camp along with metal fragments of the plane. With makeshift soldering tools, the coin was heated and welded to a small band of the plane's metal to form a ring. Forged from the embers of war and the sacrifice of a young American pilot, the small silver ring,

---

[19] *The Library of Congress World War II Companion*. (2007). New York: Simon & Schuster, 623.

with the prophetic word "liberty," found a waiting place in Ed's pocket.

At the same time, Ed felt an urgency to see Ivet. The war was now escalating out of control. Either one of them could lose their life in an instant, just like that pilot.

My father was always a person void of ulterior motives and he had little salesmanship about him. Consequently, he had a very pure sense of generosity. Still, in the burnt-out hills of Kobe, he had nothing to give Ivet, nothing except this small token of love and his heart that had now been captured and taken prisoner.

The Silver Ring. Photo of the ring my father made for my mother in 1945.

Love Escapes the Ruins

The cones of certain pine trees will only open with the heat of a forest fire. It is a profound thing to find life and love emerge from the ruins of war.

※

As a student of literature, I recall the studies of Dante's *Divine Comedy* and my professor's exposé on the notion of *felix culpa*, Adam and Eve's "fortunate fall." That out of something terrible came something good. For Adam and Eve, their ban from the Garden would, consequently, lead to a promise of redemption in the Advent of Christ.

However one chooses to define the conditions of Kobe in the summer of 1945, it was certainly a fall from the grace of life to be living there whether you were American, Turkish, or Japanese. The joy of this story and the reason for telling it is the ultimate fortune that two people found while in this fallen state of war. How would, against all odds, one find beauty in such an incinerated hell, much less love?

But Ed had found love with someone who had by now, more than once, kept him from going hungry. During all the secret runs back and forth, Ed and Ivet had kindled quite a growing romance.

Still, as far as the war went, the summer of 1945 had proven to be perhaps the lowest point for Ed and Ivet as well as millions of others. The images of her torched neighborhood were horrifying for Ivet. And Ed, back at camp, was losing weight and becoming ill again. This, however, soon became juxtaposed with a setting that transported the two of them literally and figuratively above the horrific fray.

Their romance was spared the ultimate horrors of the war while a sense of urgency grew. For the men, every raid drained more of their supplies. For the women, it was a race against time to get supplies to the ones they loved—perhaps, for the last time.

Kobe, Japan 1945. Shamil captured this view of a decimated Kobe seen from the hills of Futatabi. Front and center, standing nearly alone, the city's only mosque with its signature turrets was spared bombing and survived the heavy air raids.

By the 1st of July, Ed's penmanship was noticeably weakened as he noted food for the men amounted to *3 spoons per man 3 times a day*. By the next month, he was back down to 147 pounds and yet somehow, he and

Woody were secretly meeting the girls at least twice a month during that summer. Literally, picnics in the hills.

Woody recalled one picnic in particular, planned for the first week in August. Both he and Ed were mad. Due to their poor health, the two of them had come down with conjunctivitis, so-called "pink eye," a frustrating turn of events due to its potentially contagious nature only days before the picnic.

By now Naila's sister Aisha had sparked a romance with Ed's good friend Zane Stickel. Sometimes a couple met here, another couple met there, but for this particular picnic, all six were getting together: Ed and Ivet, Woody and Naila, Zane and Aisha.

It has to be the most diametrically opposed image to this whole story to know that as the couples were innocently preparing picnic lunches on that August day, American forces were simultaneously completing military coordinates for the single most devastating air raid in the history of mankind. On the same day the couples were heading to their picnic, August 6, 1945, 150 miles south of Kobe, the entire city of Hiroshima was struck and virtually annihilated by the first atomic bomb ever detonated on a civilian population in human history. 100,000 people were killed instantly—among them American prisoners of war as well. Less than 10 percent of the city's buildings survived.

Immediate word of the devastation never reached the couples. Ed and Woody made no reference to Hiroshima in their diaries. Stranger still is that there was little reference to the event three days later when in Nagasaki yet another atomic bomb flattened 43 square miles of the city, instantly killing another 70,000 Japanese.

Woody only noted hearing radio news of a new state of war between the Soviet Union and Japan, some mention of a nearby raid at Amagasaki, and a news article discussing *the horrors of some new bomb the Americans are using*. Still unaware, the men scheduled yet another picnic for August 11th.

Finally by the 11th, Woody wrote that *the news up front is becoming almost quiet enough to be called ominous. The Japanese are really moaning about the use of some new terror bomb. They protest it is worse than gas and even less humane.*

The men began speculating that the war might be winding down but they never found out, until much later, the gravity of what had just occurred. Unbeknownst to the couples, Hiroshima and Nagasaki sat virtually desolate as they went about their secret summer getaways.

Their last picnic in August ended up being a quick meeting. Years before the war, Baba had acquired a cabin in Arima, which is located in the hills above Kobe but is much farther north than Futatabi. Just prior to this picnic, the girls had been staying at the cabin. Finding the men's camp from Arima was going to be more difficult so the girls asked Sam to help them. Because of the distance, the girls would not be able to visit with the boys for very long.

Ivet recalled, "It was a short rendezvous and the boys decided to walk back with us halfway. I remember, at one point, we all had to duck and hide as we came across a bunch of soldiers. It was at that point that we decided to say goodbye to the boys."

While I never learned of the exact time and place when Ed gave Ivet his ring, I do know it was very soon after it was made. Knowing how shy my father could be, it wouldn't have surprised me if he agonized and fumbled with it over a long walk just like this one and would have waited to the very end to reach into his pocket and offer the ring to my mother.

Years later when I asked Mother whether she considered it to be an engagement ring or a going-steady ring, she simply said, "Well, it was a ring that said 'Be mine.'" After many walks through the trails and heartbeats of the Kobe hills, Ed's ring ultimately found its true home on the hand of his treasured nightingale during the consuming and rapturous summer days of 1945 on that charred island of Japan.

Hundreds of thousands of people were being killed. Ports and cities were in ashes. Atom bombs were falling from the sky. Ed was ill and virtually starving. Despite all that, my mother and father were falling in love with each other—on secret picnics in the hills of Kobe.

PART SIX: FREEDOM

War Ends: Ed Meets Safa

T**he war ends and Ed meets a remarkable stranger as he searches for Ivet. What Ed later discovers leaves him speechless.**

※※※

Reportedly, Truman had more atomic bomb sites planned after Nagasaki. Many have speculated that Kobe was certainly on the list, in which case the story of Ed and Ivet could have easily ended here. Thankfully, it did not end for them and millions of others—including me!

After their last short picnic, Ivet and the girls returned to the cabin to spend the rest of the week together. That summer they had seen the men more often than at any other time. Now—having become thoroughly intoxicated with their American romances—the girls had hours to speculate over what the future would hold. And while the girls were still madly and foolishly in love, they were also gravely worried about the men's deteriorating health and the raids that frayed the prisoners' ever-thinning lines of food supply. It was at this time that Ivet heard news from the Emperor coming over the radio.

"I remember the girls and I were still at the cabin when we were listening to the radio. Emperor Hirohito came on. We all ran over close to listen. I remember he began telling his people that the war was over. We started screaming and yelling. You have no idea how happy we were. We wasted no time. We stopped everything we were doing, packed our things, and got on the next train home.

"When I got home, Mother was alone and so happy to see us. She was fixing a special dinner, whatever she could get together, to celebrate. The next day, I wanted to quickly go meet up with Ed. I put my things together and asked Mother if I could go out. Well, that morning, Mother had found out about our adventures. She was furious with me, so mad she took my shoes away and told me to go up to my room."

"Bar uz bulmängä! Kilgäch atanga äytermen!" ("You go to your room! I will tell your father when he gets home!")

Who could blame Aba? This was, after all, wartime. Especially by now, Ivet was risking life and limb in negotiating the endless raids to see her man. At 21, she was still far too young, in her mother's eyes, to be concerning herself with a foreigner 10 years older than she and outside the faith no less. Like her daughter, Maksura also cultivated a protective streak toward her loved ones. While Maksura believed in love, there was also a part of her who was not averse to arranging relationships for her children. Not a hard and fast rule but certainly a preference to that of falling madly in love with some forlorn and beleaguered prisoner of war. In any case, upstairs she went! Ivet was banned to her room. And without her shoes!

Needless to say, at camp the word of the war ending ignited absolute pandemonium. One can imagine the explosive revelry. Further, authorities were not only instructed to lay down their arms but *to safeguard, at all costs, the lives of prisoners of war and internees,* according to Woody.

The next day, just as Ivet was being sent to her room, Ed had made a beeline for Kobe. He soon found himself in an encounter, the odds of which cannot be found in a bookie's office or department of probability and statistics or any other chance under the moon or stars that I can possibly imagine.

Ed went frantically looking for Ivet. One can only imagine what he looked like by then, ill and underfed. He must have told us the story a hundred times of when he walked by a mirror and waved to himself. He'd become so skinny he didn't recognize his own reflection. What he also barely recognized was what had once been downtown Kobe as he attempted to trace his way back towards what was now the ruins of the Marks House. In the distance Ed could see the Kobe Mosque still standing and recalled that Ivet's food center was near there. Stopping to talk to people, he described Ivet. Did they know her, perhaps her community? Getting vague descriptions of where he believed Ivet's neighborhood was, Ed headed back up the hill.

Kobe Mosque 1945. Ed searched for Ivet in the ruins of Kobe and there stumbled upon the surprise of his life. Photo: www.kobemosque.org/History

Meanwhile, Baba had left home and was heading down hill. In all the streets of Kobe and of all the hundreds and thousands of human beings left in that city, roaming about celebrating and scavenging, two men of families with roots as far apart as could possibly be met by chance. One on his way up the hill, the other on his way down. Neither knew each other from Adam but there they were. They stopped to talk.

Ed explained to Safa who he was and that he was desperately looking for his fiancée and might Safa know her or where she lived. Because Safa was not fluent in English, he only partially understood what Ed was saying. He did not fully realize Ed was, in fact, looking for his daughter! What Safa could understand was that Ed was hot and perspiring, looked like he hadn't had a decent meal in months, and was either lost or in need of some kind of help. Safa was the kind of man whose generous nature and instinctive hospitality easily overruled the need to understand all the details. He insisted that Ed simply come to his home where he could feed him, calm him down, and try to help him out.

"Pop was always inviting strangers over. It seemed like an endless array of people sometimes," Rashid once recalled. This would, however, be one stranger unlike any other.

In the meantime, Farida had also headed out the door. She was on her way to get exchange rations and planned to stop by Aba's to see Ivet. She had a lot to be worried about as well. In the last couple of weeks, Farida had discovered what Ivet's little tent set-up was all about. Ivet finally spilled the beans to Farida one day, telling her that she and the girls had been going up to Futatabi to smuggle food to the prisoners, which is why they needed the tent as a stopping point. Farida remembered her short and heated conversation with Ivet.

"Sin tilerdeŋme? Totsalar?" ("Are you crazy? What if they catch you?")

"Min kurkmim, anı yaratam!" ("I don't care, I love him!")

From then on Farida was very frightened for Ivet, sensing from the tone that this was one of those times not to stand in Ivet's way, much less try to change her mind.

Meanwhile, Ivet couldn't sit still. Sheepishly she ventured out of her room. From the top of the stairs and in a surge of emotions, she pleaded with Aba. The two exchanged words and soon Ivet's pleading turned to arguing, which rather than persuading her mother simply further angered her. Frustrated, Aba shouted again for her to go to her room. And then the unbelievable happened.

"Just then the door opened. From atop the stairway, I could see it was Dad. He'd brought someone home with him. It was Ed! I couldn't believe it. What in the world was he doing here, I thought? You have no idea how surprised I was. Well, Mother had to invite him in and called me down to help. I was shaking. Mother made tea. I remember poor Ed having to drink tea on this hot day in the middle of summer. You know how he is with hot tea. Of course, we didn't have any ice. He had an Army handkerchief. Sitting there wiping his forehead, dripping with perspiration but was pleased to have the tea and cookies."

Ed had every right to perspire. Trekking up and down the hills of Kobe in the dead heat of August, then being served tea. Then suddenly realizing he was smack-dab in the lioness's den having been escorted there, no less, by the unsuspecting father of the woman he was, up to now, deeply but secretly in love with. It's a wonder he didn't faint then and there. His pale complexion was no doubt the result of hunger, the family must have imagined. At some point Ed was perspiring so badly, they offered to have Ivet wash his shirt—just as Farida walked in the door.

"That day I stopped in at Mom's house. What I didn't know was that Ed had met Baba quite by chance. By the time they'd climbed the hill to Baba's house, Ed's shirt was all wet. When I arrived at the house, Ivet was just coming downstairs with Ed's shirt. I saw Ed in the middle of the living room half dressed, thin and very tall."

Farida pulled Ivet aside and whispered, "Bu kem?" ("Who is that?")

"Bu tege yeget kaysın min yaratam." ("That's the guy I told you I fell in love with.") Ivet went on whispering that she was still learning how Safa and Ed had run into each other and how Safa had ended up bringing him there!

I have often thought how true the adage applied to Ed that "if he didn't have bad luck, he would have never had any luck at all." Only hours after being freed as a captured prisoner of war, part of him must have certainly felt suddenly a captured and pinned prisoner of love. In this type of situation, Ed was not particularly good at explaining things, off the cuff. He never had the gift of gab. He was much better meeting challenges with planning and strategy. Realizing he did not possess snake oil talents, Ed would have accepted that his best chance was simply the truth.

Fortunately, however, the truth could wait. Maksura and Safa, after all, still could not understand English very well. For now, translated pleasantries and hospitalities could continue to veil the secret romance while Ed and Ivet shared disbelieving stares and tried to figure out how they would, figuratively, drop yet another bomb on this household.

"From that day on, Ed came every day bringing all kinds of food, medicine, and whatever he could get his hands on. Right after the war ended, planes flew low and dropped big barrels of these items into the boys' camp. They had all kinds of things. It was said that some of the guys actually got hurt trying to catch the barrels coming down through their roofs. Your father continued courting me and one day asked me to marry him. Well, this was never done, marrying outside our religion. So, it was very hard trying to convince my parents that I loved him and I wanted to marry him," Ivet recalled.

And so, with proposal in hand, Ivet approached her busy parents, took them aside, sat them down, and spilled the beans—in her native tongue. The noisy, clamoring, chatty living room chilled. As she expected, this was a bomb that dropped hard and then was followed by a similar hush of shocked silence. The war no longer mattered. Peace no longer mattered. There was suddenly a new and enormous issue facing this family as reality grabbed Safa's and Maksura's attention.

Battle lines would soon be drawn. On the one side was my mother, a gentle loving soul who was, nevertheless, boldly determined alongside a somewhat disheveled, tall, skinny albeit sincere foreigner. On the other side was custom, protocol, and the traditions of a family's faith embodied in the hearts and minds of Safa and Maksura, perhaps slightly more deeply in that of Maksura. Tilting the scale further were what Sam liked to call "the Council," which included the combined sentiments of Maksura and two rather angry aunts.

At least by now the family had gotten to know a little about this American who was, after all, lavishing them daily with gifts from above. But would that be enough?

Imperial Rescript

To Our good and loyal subjects:

After pondering deeply the general trends of the world and the actual conditions in Our Empire today, We have decided to effect a settlement of the present situation by resorting to an extraordinary measure.

We have ordered Our Government to communicate to the Governments of the United States, Great Britain, China, and the Soviet Union that Our Empire accepts the provisions of their Joint Declaration.

To strive for the common prosperity and happiness of all nations as well as the security and well-being of Our subjects is the solemn obligation which has been handed down by Our Imperial Ancestors, and which We hold close to heart. Indeed, We declared war on America and Britain out of Our sincere desire to ensure Japan's self-preservation and stabilization of East Asia, it being far from Our thought either to infringe upon the sovereignty of other nations or to embark upon territorial aggrandizement. But now the war has lasted for nearly four years. Despite the best that has been done by everyone—the gallant fighting of military and naval forces, the diligence and assiduity of Our servants of the State, and the devoted service of Our 100-million people, the war situation has developed not necessarily to Japan's advantage, while the general trends of the world have all turned against her interests. Moreover, the enemy has begun to employ a new and most cruel bomb, the power of which to do damage is indeed incalculable, taking the toll of many innocent lives. Should We continue to fight, it would not only result in an ultimate collapse and obliteration of the Japanese nation, but also it would lead to the total extinction of human civilization. Such being the case, how are We to save the millions of Our subjects, or to atone Ourselves before the hallowed spirit of Our Imperial Ancestors? This is the reason why We have ordered the acceptance of the provisions of the Joint Declaration of the Powers.

We cannot but express the deepest sense of regret to Our allied nations of East Asia, who have consistently cooperated with the Empire towards the emancipation of East Asia. The thought of those officers and men as well as others who have fallen in the fields of battle, those who died at their post of duty, or those who met an untimely death and all their bereaved families, pains Our heart night and day. The welfare of the wounded and the war sufferers, and of those who have lost their home and livelihood, are the objects of Our profound solicitude. The hardships and sufferings to which Our nation is to be subjected hereafter will be certainly great. We are keenly aware of the inmost feelings of all ye, Our subjects. However, it is according to the dictates of time and fate that We have resolved to pave the way for a grand peace for all the generations to come by enduring the unendurable and suffering what is insufferable.

Having been able to safeguard and maintain the structure of the Imperial State, We are always with ye, Our good and loyal subjects, relying upon your sincerity and integrity. Beware most strictly of any outbursts of emotion which may engender needless complications, or any fraternal contention and strife which may create confusion, lead ye astray, and cause ye to lose the confidence of the world. Let the entire nation continue as one family from generation to generation, ever firm in its faith of the imperishableness of its divine land, and mindful of its heavy burden of responsibilities, and the long road before it. Unite your total strength to be devoted to the construction for the future. Cultivate the ways of rectitude; foster nobility of spirit; and work with resolution so as ye may enhance the innate glory of the Imperial State and keep pace with the progress of the world.

(Imperial Sign Manual)
(Imperial Seal)

August 14, 1945.
Emperor Hirohito's statement of surrender.
The Mainichi, Osaka, Japan.

Ed and Ivet Marry

BEFORE LEAVING JAPAN, ED, WOODY, AND ZANE ENGAGE IN A MOSLEM CEREMONY AND A TRIP TO KYOTO.

"When Ivet broke the news about the marriage, Aba went crazy," Sam recalled. It was not only that her daughter had been disobeying her all this time by venturing out in such dangerous conditions but Aba was having a tough time with one obvious issue: marriage outside the faith.

I would describe my grandparents as sophisticated, tolerant, worldly, unusually generous and hospitable and, at the same time, deeply religious people. Their faith was private but strong as steel. And so it was a very difficult thing for Maksura to relinquish a part of her tradition. This was a woman who, as a young teenager, had traveled across the plains of Russia to find a new home in Harbin. Then, she traveled further to raise a family in yet another foreign country, only to later face another pummeling war. It is thus no surprise that Maksura held close to the traditions of her family—the food, the language, and certainly the faith among all these changes in her life—to maintain some sense of sanity. Naturally Maksura put up quite a fight for her tradition of marriage. And, for that matter, while Safa was clearly a man of the world, he also conducted prayer services at the Mosque on occasion and, in terms of his faith, he was unwavering as well.

But my father did have a ray of hope. Ivet's family had had to assimilate many cultures in their migrating life, which required understanding and respecting varying traditions. Likewise, my father was raised by a physician who took an oath in a profession that insisted upon mercy for all people, regardless of their origin. Neither of these families had the luxury of cloistered fundamentalism. Both families valued their faith but, practically speaking, they were always steered away from doing so fanatically. And so, my father faced a possibility with Ivet's family because at the end of the day there was a shared sentiment in the world views of these respective families, who—among other things—valued the trust, love, and promises of an individual found to be authentic.

The "Council" was soon called to a meeting with Safa. The Council of three included Maksura, her sister Aziza, and Aisha's and Naila's mother Mahira. Farida was there as interpreter while the four adults hammered Ed with a barrage of questions. The odds were clearly stacked against Ed. By all accounts, the closed door meetings lasted quite some time.

In the end, Ivet was quite surprised to find Safa emerge to announce she would be allowed to marry Ed after all. First, what Safa saw was an honest man. A veteran tradesman himself, Safa could have but did not spot any snake oil in Ed's answers. In addition, Ed was from a well-off family as Safa himself had been. Ed also loved horses and dreamed of a ranch some day in the States. Safa's father had also raised horses. In short, Ed was credible. While my dad could be a wisecracker under stress, there was a "Jimmy Stewart" quality about him—non-threatening, endearing, and clearly resourceful. He was a decent man genuinely in love with their daughter and he was from a country that had just won the war.

It was a huge step for Safa and Maksura. Never before had anyone in their family married outside the faith. Clearly, the other girls were persuasive also because not only was Ivet granted permission, Naila and Aisha were as well. The mood of the household quickly changed from somber to celebratory. Once the decision was made, there was no turning back on anyone's part. The date for the wedding was set for August 28, 1945, a triple wedding—Ed and Ivet, Woody and Naila, Zane and Aisha.

The wedding was held at Safa's home. In postwar fashion, Ivet's white satin wedding dress was made by her next-door neighbor in exchange for 10 pounds of sugar. Ed had to borrow clothes from Rashid even though the sleeves of the suit were too short and Rashid's size 10 shoes were a tight fit for Ed's size 12 feet. During rehearsals, Rashid recalled taking the three men up to his room to practice the ceremony, translating for the Mullah. Apparently, the Mullah only got confused once, nearly marrying Naila to Ed. Other than that and despite the language barrier, the wedding went off beautifully.

Before leaving the country, the couples managed to take a quick honeymoon to Kyoto. Not only was Kyoto fairly close to Kobe, it is believed the city was spared bombing due to its number of historic temples and palaces. Ivet recalled their trip with humor.

"While in Kyoto, we went to City Hall explaining that the men were American reporters. We asked for a car. The only cars available were those of high officials. We snuck over and took one. I had my little American flag, the one I got during the 4th of July fairs at the port festivals. I attached it to the car. It looked very official. We drove this way all over. Everyone we passed by saluted us as though there were generals in the car.

"We stayed at the Miyako Hotel for about a week. One morning we were awakened to knocking on the door. Ed was half-asleep. The knocking startled him; he bolted out of bed, forgetting that the war was over. It turned out it was the hotel attendants simply asking for the list of things we wanted. Ed rubbed his forehead, regained himself, and responded by telling them we wanted steaks and bread and also toilet paper—and gasoline. These were things you normally could not find anywhere. I don't know where they got it all, but they did. We were star-struck the whole time and being treated like kings and queens."

Turkish Brides. An unforgettable wedding day for three Turkish brides. (L to R) My mother Ivet and her cousins Naila and Aisha.

August 28, 1945. (L to R) Ed, Ivet, Woody, Naila, Zane, and Aisha in their triple wedding held at Ivet's home. My father stands a far cry from his 201-pound stature before the war. Ivet's dress cost Safa 10 pounds of sugar.

Area Prisoners Win Turkish Brides in Jap Camp Romances

Two From S. F., One From Berkeley, Wait First Chance to Come Home

By BONNIE WILEY

YOKOHAMA, Sept. 9. — (Delayed) — (AP) — Three bright-eyed brides sat on an ancient dusty suitcase in front of the Yokohama dock warehouse which the Forty-second General Hospital is using to process prisoners of war.

They were happy because they hope to be able to go to San Francisco with their husbands, whom they married in Kobe after prison camp romances.

An amazing story of courtships carried on behind guards' backs and over a prison camp fence was revealed. Two of the girls, daughters of a Turkish importer, are sisters. The third is their cousin. Two were born in Japan and the third in China. All speak English fluently. They learned the language in a Canadian academy in Japan.

BAY AREA MEN.

They are Ivet Bacon, 21, married to H. Edward Bacon, 5 Roca Way, San Francisco; Nalla Woodruff, 18, married to Arthur Woodruff, 2709 Dwight Way, Berkeley, and Aisha Stickel, 22, married to Zane Allen Stickel, 70 Cedro Way, San Francisco.

Stickel said:

"We all met while we three men were civilians working for the Navy on Guam and were captured in December, 1941. We were interned in the Kobe civilian camp. The girls, being Turkish, were not interned. The ration dump where we all got food was just four doors from our camp and we met the girls when they came for food.

"We talked to them every day when they came for food and they smuggled black market food to us. To meet them, we climbed the prison camp fence.

RUSH WEDDING.

"At first we planned to be married in September, but when the war was over and prisoners of war were being moved out, we decided to be married immediately in the hope our wives could be taken to the States with us.

"We were married by a Turkish priest at an elaborate ceremony arranged by the girls' relatives. The brides were able to buy material for wedding dresses for ten pounds of sugar and 100 yen. The ceremony was nice, despite war conditions.

"We all went to Kyoto on a honeymoon, but when we heard prisoners of war were moving out so fast, we decided to come here. We are not sure we will be able to take the girls back to San Francisco. But we are sure trying."

RISKY COURTSHIP.

Their secret meetings during courtship were not too safe, Woodruff said:

"One time I jumped over the fence to meet Nalla and was caught by a guard. I was thrown into jail for a week and Nalla was slapped around."

"But I didn't cry," Nalla interrupted.

All three girls are attractive, although they have had no new clothes for four years. Two are blondes and the third is a sparkling brunette. Every time San Francisco was mentioned, the three broke into broad smiles and said how much they hoped to be able to go to the United States.

September 1945. News reaches San Francisco of the triple wedding as reported by this Associated Press article.

Complications in the Philippines

The couples finally set sail for the Philippines. In Manila, while being processed to return to the United States, Ed is refused entry.

※❀※

While in Kyoto, the couples heard news that American troops were beginning to land and many of the POWs were starting to leave the island. The men felt anxious to get moving. Ed and Ivet soon found themselves in the port of Yokohama looking for a ship heading to the States. Ivet remembered how they secured transport on the *USS Tryon*.

"We got to the docks but could not get on any of the ships. The transports were all full of prisoner-of-war men and there were no accommodations for women. The boys didn't know what to do. They went asking one captain after another if they could bring their wives. They all said no. Finally, one of the sergeants listened to our problem and told us, 'Just take them aboard.' So we snuck on. Once we got there, the captain was so nice. He gave us girls the medic's quarters. The boys went with the rest of the troops all in one big cabin.

"It seemed there were hundreds on board. As we were the only women on the ship, all six of us were invited to eat with the captain and his staff.

The food was out of this world after being hungry for so long, especially for the boys."

News of the triple wedding was beginning to get press, and by September the story had reached the Bay Area. Ed's sister Marge was living in an apartment in San Francisco. Lucylle lived in the same building, a floor below Marge. Both were now clueless as to Ed's condition or whereabouts. Needless to say, when the Associated Press called Lucylle's apartment asking about a triple marriage, which included an H. Edward Bacon, Marge nearly dropped a brick.

"I happened to answer the phone and I didn't want Mother to hear the conversation. I asked them to transfer the call upstairs. Mother was still writing Ed, but we really didn't know if he was dead or alive at this point. When they called back, I insisted they tell me what they knew and then I'd tell them what I knew."

"I finally went downstairs to talk to Mother. She asked if they'd confirmed anything. I told her they said he was alive and … he'd married a Turkish gal. 'Well, I don't know who she is but I'm sure if Ed married her, she's a fine girl,' Mother said. After hearing that Ed's new wife was Turkish, both Mother and I naïvely imagined Ivet to be a black woman, draped with a veil."

By mid-September the couples arrived in the Philippines. According to Woody, they were taken about eight miles south of Manila to the WRDC (Women's Replacement and Disposition Center). There the couples were processed: physicals, de-licing, endless paperwork, and interrogations. Ivet recalled they wanted to know how the prisoners had been treated, where were they from, what were they doing before they were captured, who were the women, and where are they going? She also said the food was very good and that they all gained a lot of weight. "I think the idea was to fatten the men up before they sent them home," she said.

The couples shared their meals and were able to stay together all day. But at bedtime the couples were required to be separated even though they were married. The girls stayed with the nurses.

During this process in Manila, Ed ran into some unexpected trouble. It seemed his marriage to Arlene was still on the books. Final papers had never been filed. Sporting this new wife, authorities deemed Ed a bigamist and refused to allow him to reenter the United States until he could show proof of divorce. This Jimmy Stewart quickly grew a short fuse and Ed immediately shot off a telegram home urging his sister Marge to find and send his old divorce papers, quickly.

"So then I get a telegram from the Philippines, 'Need divorce papers. Please take care of this!'" Marge recalled. "At the time Eddie [Davis] and I were engaged but he was in Arabia, Dad had passed away, my sister Connie was out of town, and I didn't want to bother Mother. I didn't have anyone to turn to. I went to the Immigration Office to explain. They said I had to show divorce papers. I didn't know what to do. I finally went to an attorney."

Within a week Oakland attorney Leo Murcell of Goldwater & Murcell drafted specific instructions for Ed in a letter dated September 26, 1945.

[Enclosed is] a rough form of an affidavit, which you may take as a guide, inserting those dates you are familiar with and adding pertinent data that may be helpful. If you will go to an attorney in Manila and have him prepare the affidavit in English along the lines we have indicated and have the same acknowledged before a notary public, whose commission is authenticated in the manner explained above, and return this to us, together with the affidavit for final, by air mail, we will make an application before the Judge of the Superior Court of the City and County of San Francisco, who will date back your final decree of divorce to June 25, 1942, the date you could have legally obtained it. In this manner your present marriage will have become legal.

One can just imagine Ed's face reading Leo's words. Ed may have exemplified the Jimmy Stewart profile of kindheartedness, but he was a very proud man as well. To read that his marriage to Ivet was anything but legal no doubt sent him through the roof, much less put him in the mood for bureaucratic calisthenics to prove that it was.

Unfortunately, this was all due to the fact that Ed's earlier Interlocutory Divorce—one that allows for a cooling-off period—was never followed up by either Ed or Arlene with papers to finalize the divorce. What Leo was trying to do was to prepare a case of *Nunc pro tunc* ("now for then") in which a court would grant the divorce retroactively. Apparently this was a common practice following Interlocutory Divorces where someone simply forgets to file a final decree. In the days ahead, Ed ultimately followed Leo's instructions and sent off the required paperwork and then set to pacing the floor.

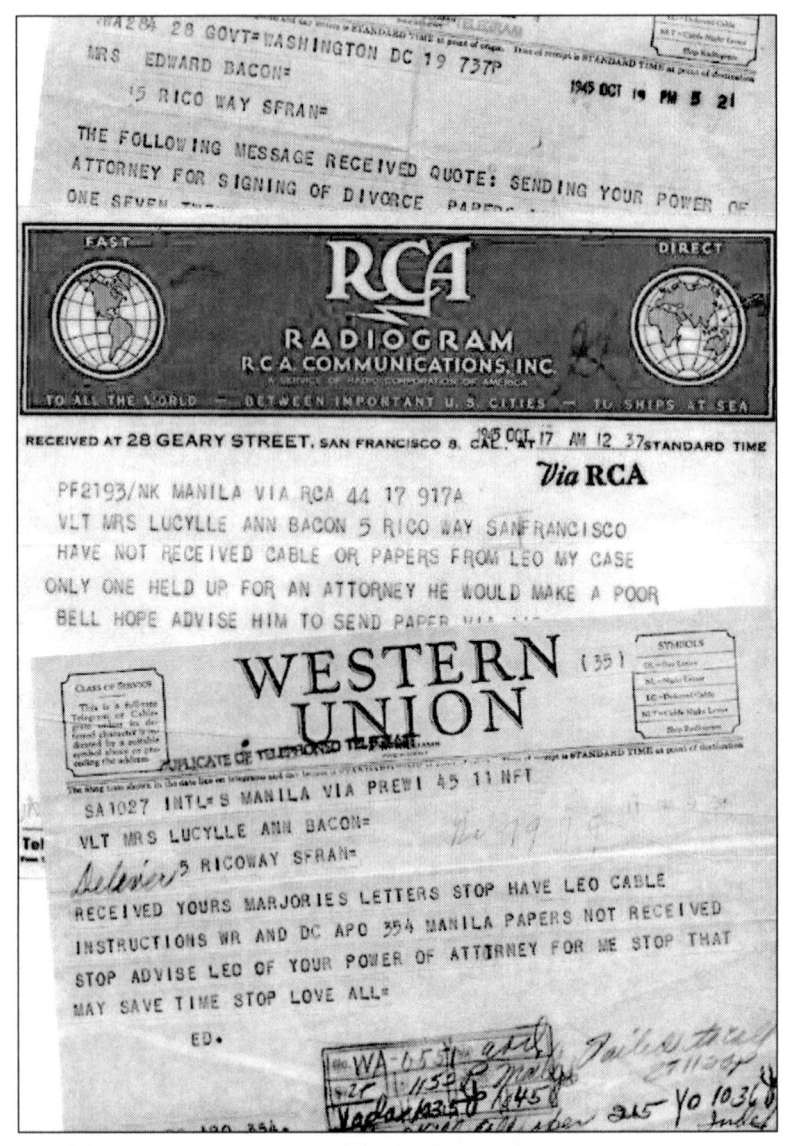

Trying times. Ed spent weeks in Manila sending scores of telegrams like these in an effort to clear the way for his return.

Journey Home

USNS General John Pope (T-AP-110) ca. 1950
Department of Navy, Naval Historical Center, Photo NH #104267.

Truman ends the war but it is Marge who finally parts the seas for Ed and Ivet.

In the end it was not surprising to find Marge picking up the slack in this absurd process to get Ed home. My father's sister actually proved to be Ed's closest and lifelong friend. We all knew her as *Auntie Marge*. She was a cross between Rosalind Russell's Auntie Mame and 40s' icon Ava Gardner. When I was visiting her in the hospital two weeks before she died, she leaned over and whispered to me, "Two ladies outside the hall in their wheelchairs absolutely made my day. I heard one of them say to the other, 'Do you know there is a movie star in that room?'" It was a touching moment for her at a time when she was very aware that the stakes were up for her, as well as a kind testament to her ageless beauty.

While my father remained a rascal all his life, Marge reminded us from "whence" he came. Marge was the picture of "class." But she was equally down to earth and never minced words. One time she described the choice of color a neighbor painted their house as "strictly throw-up." A man's unshaven face that grew darker than a "5 o'clock shadow" was described as *shush*. "I can't stand shush on a man," she used to say. And speaking of 5 o'clock, she was quite regular with her *tidly*, which consisted of scotch on the rocks straight up. Even at the age of 50, I got dizzy trying to match her with cocktails.

Once I dropped in unexpectedly at her home in Auburn, California. Without batting an eye, she served me lunch that could have come from an upscale restaurant along with more forks and spoons than I could count.

And she was never without jewelry. One of my favorite photos is of her "relaxing" in her backyard on a summer chaise lounge doing her crossword puzzles—with a heavy set of earrings on. Only Auntie Marge, I thought.

How Marge really differed from my father was in her social skills. I could never get over the difference. She joined golf clubs, Chambers of Commerce, charities, civic clubs, and she worked on neighborhood newspapers. Compared to my father, Marge was the classic social butterfly. She often giggled while she spoke, was easily self-effacing, and a perennially polished wisecracker. Beneath all that was a woman who truly loved her "little brother," as she used to call my dad. She was quite happy in her retirement to live out her years alongside a posh Oregon golf course. Yet in her early 80s, she chose to pack things up and move to Seattle when my father's health began to take a turn for the worse. They were quite a pair, dressed up and trotting gallantly towards a restaurant door, poking fun and steadying their strides with their matching gilded canes.

The three couples' stay in Manila dragged on for weeks partly because the American Consul insisted that the wives' visas had to be cleared by the immigration authorities in Philadelphia before they could be cleared in Manila, which not only meant filing more petitions and paperwork but often having to hitchhike into town to submit the papers. In fact, it was a month before visas finally came through. While the women seemed to be taking it in stride, the men were fit to be tied.

Unfortunately, the three couples would not return to the United States together. It was all about paperwork at this point. The first to get their papers processed were Zane and Aisha, who finally caught a ride home on the *USS Lurline*. Next, Naila and Woody were cleared and caught up with the *USS Brewster*, sailing on October 18. This, of course, left unlucky Ed and Ivet.

Ex-Prisoner In S. F. With Turkish Bride

PAGE 10 CCCCAA
MONDAY, NOV. 19, 1945

Zane Allen Stickel, 30, 70 Cedro way, a former Lowell High School all-city fullback, returned yesterday to San Francisco aboard the Lurline accompanied by his Turkish wife, whom he has courted under extraordinary circumstances during the last three years in the Japanese city of Kobe.

The history of Stickel's romance begins in 1941 with his capture on Guam, where he was employed as a civilian construction worker. Because of his civilian status he was decently treated by the Japanese and shortly removed along with 50 others to internment in the Seamen's Institute Home at Kobe.

It was a year later that he first met his pretty wife, Aisha Altishe, the daughter of a Turkish exporter and importer. They met on a blind date after a friendly Japanese official had given Stickel the key to the back gate of their makeshift prison.

From then on the pair arranged frequent meetings with Stickel always successfully sneaking or walking out of the prison undetected by the ever-present guards. Although their place of internment was changed three times, Stickel said that he was always able to slip out the back door after the evening roll call to meet Aisha.

Once out on the street he was never molested by either Japanese police or civilians. It was apparently perfectly all right for him to wander around the city, go into bars or visit his fiancee. One night he even held a long conversation with members of a German submarine crew in a Kobe bar.

Mrs. Stickel, who is a devotee of Stephen Foster's songs, speaks fluent Japanese, Turkish and English. She was employed as secretary to the principal of the Canadian Academy for English-speaking students in Kobe.

Two of Stickel's companions in confinement, H. Edward Bacon of San Francisco and Arthur Woodruff of Berkeley, also made successful nightly sorties from their prison. In this way they happened to meet Aisha's cousin, Ivet, and her younger sister, Naila.

Soon there were two more American romances flourishing with attractive Turkish girls. The sum total effect was a triple Turkish wedding ceremony in Kobe at the war's end. Woodruff and his bride have already returned to the United States and the Bacons are happily on their way.

Stickel, who is husky, handsome and graying, said that last year their prison was moved to Mt. P tatabi, which rises behind Kobe. From there he had a grandstand seat from which to observe the great American fire bomb raid of March 17 which he knew would help with his liberation but which threatened the life of the girl he loved.

THEY MET IN KOBE—Mr. and Mrs. Arthur Woodruff (left), Mr. and Mrs. Zane Stickel sing "Swanee River."

November 1945. Arriving first, Woody, Naila, Zane, and Aisha receive some early press in a San Francisco newspaper. Zane recounts his clandestine courtship with Aisha during his nearly four years of internment.

For Ed, things became more complicated when communication lines broke down. Letters were getting through but, at some point, telegrams were not. This was very frustrating since so much of the paperwork was dependent on cables. Nearly a month had gone by, and Ed still had not heard back from the lawyer Leo Murcell at which point he took out his frustrations by referring to Leo as a *poor bellhop* in one telegram.

"I'd send telegrams telling Ed I was working on getting him his papers only to find the telegraphs were down," Marge recalled. "He never got my messages and, instead, kept sending pleading telegrams. Connie and I agreed to keep the details from Mother. Ed's imprisonment had taken such a toll on her over the years. So, while Connie, Louis, Leo, and I were scrambling like crazy, we pretended everything was moving smooth as clockwork if Mother asked. In the meantime, I went to the library to learn all about Turkish women."

About this time, Ed's sister Connie sent a letter off trying to calm Ed down by explaining frustrations from their side of the ocean.

Marge and I have chased around like mad getting papers. Louis has talked to Leo and everyone is trying. If you ever catch up with all the papers that have been sent you, you wouldn't be able to carry them in a pickup truck. Mother is sleeping again after 4 years. She looks better already. She has aged greatly since you saw her. Marge and I have agreed to see to it that she only gets good news.

Despite my aunts' good intentions, the truth is that my grandmother was anything but a sleeping log. She knew exactly what was going on and, quite frankly, she started out the month of October giving Ed quite a mouthful. She began one letter, *I'm not scolding you,* then proceeded to do precisely that. She urged him to stop being bitter and to think of his new wife, suspecting that every time he cultivated bitterness, that it must make Ivet unhappy also. She added that those in the U.S. had sacrificed quite a bit as well, informing him that people *have been taxed very high with bonds that were taken out of workers paychecks—before they could even draw their pay—[but that was what] gave us all the equipment with which we won the fight.* She went on to remind him, *true there is red tape, always was and always will be, but this is still a grand place to live.* Finally, she cautioned him that returning to the U.S. with bitterness *would give you a bad start since everyone here in the country is pretty well edgy themselves.*

Eventually Ed was starting to get the picture as communication lines improved. On October 14, Lucylle sent another letter to Ed bringing things further into perspective but with the kind of wisdom and comfort only a mother knows how to dish out.

So glad to receive pictures. Ivet resembles Mrs. Barngrover.... I liked her before but her smiling eyes have endeared her that much more to me. I know she has been a great comfort to you. That's a cute wedding picture of the two of you. It breaks my heart to look at you in the picture and think of what the horrible experience has done to you. But now you are free and I know you will be alright within a short time. At least they didn't take that smile away from you.... I hope you are getting good food and are gaining weight. My poor dears you will just have to relax and be as calm as possible because Washington doesn't seem to be in a terrible rush about getting you home.... I am so anxious for you to return without bitterness in your heart. Every family here has been affected one way or another. And those married in England and Australia have had similar delays.... Anyway it will be grand when you get here. We have turkey waiting for you. Loads of love to you both. Mother.

While Ed continued to struggle with his frustrating dilemma, his mother's words hit a cord. Venting could only take someone so far. His tone softened as he reflected on his mother's letters and his new wife—treasures that drew him above the fray.

I hope we can be home for Christmas this year. The happiest Christmas I ever had was the one in 1943. Many of the men received personal packages and I got a letter you had sent. It was a great Christmas even though I was a prisoner. That letter meant more to me than any Xmas gift I ever received. I don't think I'll ever receive one that will mean as much as that one did.... I think Ivet is writing you a letter right now. To answer your question, no she hasn't heard from her family. No mail is being sent to Japan yet so there's not much chance of hearing from them. It's been hard on the girls since we left Japan but they have been very good about it. I've really got a good wife this time. Thanksgiving looks out of the question but we will be thinking of you. Please don't worry. Edd

Thanks to Marge, Thanksgiving would not necessarily be out of the question. Frustrated with this whole process, Auntie Marge made a bold move.

"Finally, I called Governor Warren's office. I told them this was an emergency and that the Immigration Office would only release Ed if a decree was issued retroactive to the original divorce date. Eventually I got the Governor to send those documents, which is what finally allowed Ed to come home."

That and a few forged signatures by the time she was finished, according to Marge. On November 2, the much coveted Final Judgment of Divorce arrived in Manila, setting the couple free at last. It had been nearly two months since they had left Japan. Five days later Ed and Ivet boarded the *USS Pope* bound for San Francisco.

"The ship that took us to the States was full of dispatched Army Nurses and WACs," Ivet remembered. "Again, I had to bunk with the nurses but they were very nice. I was so naïve. They showed me a lot of things. They were the ones who taught me how to properly shave my legs and pluck my eyebrows and cut my hair. They made me a new person."

As for Ed, the *USS Pope* made him a new person as well. The movement with the sea beneath him was delirium in its best form. After nearly four years, it was finally over. His soul at peace, he could now celebrate with the ship's best wine and the sounds of "Sentimental Journey," his Turkish bride wrapped in his arms sailing with him, back to his home, to his Golden Gate, to his familiar and embracing Frisco fog, his loving mother and anxious sisters, to those turkey dinners, chocolate cakes, and cherry pies, to his Land of Plenty. Ed could allow himself, for the first time, to embrace the joy of freedom upon this transport, which gently carved a path through the Pacific, free of obstacles and the contentious pace of war.

Because of their delay, Ed and Ivet arrived quite a bit later than the other couples but their landing was, perhaps, all the more special. After years of captivity and a Homeric voyage across the seas, Ed and his new bride arrived in San Francisco—appropriately—on Thanksgiving Day, November 22, 1945, to the confetti and cheers of their family and friends.

I once asked my mother if she'd had other boyfriends. She did and was proud to tell me that one in particular was from a very rich family, a European, who'd lived in Shioya near the French Consul's home where she'd worked. But, she said, he wasn't around when times got tough.

"When I returned home, I became busy helping your father and I started to care for him."

In the end, she picked Ed because she instinctively knew he would bring her that home that she used to always point to when she would tell her mother *that's* where I want to live someday. She also found a home in the heart of someone who, while self-sufficient in so many ways, demonstrated he was also a man who desperately needed and loved her. Those truths never changed.

And Ed picked Ivet because in his most vulnerable of times, he finally reached out in hope and trust to someone who, in turn, not only poignantly sacrificed herself and her safety for his survival but in the process allowed him to reap the best life had to offer. In the worst of times, he found his greatest reward. Those truths also never changed.

If *all the world's a stage and all the men and women merely players*, I think Shakespeare would agree that these were two exceptional players. Not only did East meet West but the two fused a union as Ed and Ivet went on to enjoy 53 years of marriage.

San Francisco, November 1945, Thanksgiving Day. Connie's husband Louis (top), Grandma (Lucylle) Bacon, Connie, Marge, Ivet, and Connie's Connie-Lou and Sherry.

San Francisco Examiner 5
Friday, Nov. 23, 1945   CCCC*

12,500 ARRIVE ON TRANSPORTS

More than 12,500 military and civilian personnel from Pacific areas arrived in San Francisco yesterday to be on hand for the celebration of Thanksgiving Day.

First of a five-ship contingent to arrive was the Army transport John R. Pope with a passenger list exceeding 5,000.

Among the Pope's passengers was H. Edward Bacon Jr., 5 Rico Way, and his Turkish bride, Ivet. Bacon was one of three Bay area men who met and courted Turkish girls while they were prisoners of the Japs.

Other arrivals during the day included the Army transport General E. T. Collins, with 3,000 aboard; Allendale, with 2,000; Calvert, with 1,600, and the Bladen, with 1,000.

Due today are the Navy transport Admiral C. F. Hughes, from Manila, with approximately 5,000 passengers and the Santa Catalina with about fifty Army and Navy men.

Home at last. My parents arrive on the *USS Pope.*

Epilogue

August 1946: (L to R) Aisha, Ed, Ivet, Naila, Woody, and Zane celebrate their one-year anniversary at a San Francisco restaurant.

Naila and Woody settled in Sacramento, California, and raised a family of three children: Glenn, Neil, and Madelyn. Zane and Aisha stayed in the Bay Area moving to Burlingame, California, and raised two children: Zane and Naila.

Ed and Ivet also moved to Burlingame where they raised a family of five children: Cathy, Dena, John, me, and Michael. Eventually, all of Ivet's relatives immigrated to the United States and made their homes in the San Francisco Bay Area. Lucylle stayed in the area as well and enjoyed the company of her son and family for another 17 years until she passed away in 1962 and was laid to rest alongside her beloved Harry at Cypress Lawn Cemetery just outside San Francisco.

During the early 1960s, Safa became co-founder of the American Turko-Tatar Association of Burlingame, which was housed in a residential home converted into a community center, affectionately known as the *Bina (building)*. Today, the center still stands and serves as both an events center and mosque. Safa became a U.S. citizen two years before he died at the age of 71. While Maksura lived to the ripe age of 80 and remained surrounded by her family and community, she died having no citizenship to any country in the world. On a September afternoon in 1982, Maksura collapsed on a sidewalk in Burlingame while on her way to give a neighbor a gift of money.

Ed commuted to San Francisco for the next 30 years before retiring as a corporate security director for I. Magnin Company, a high-end retail chain. He was a consummate father, a somewhat solitary man, with a dry sense of humor and an overwhelming love for his family. He was known as "Popi" to 11 grandchildren. He and my mother followed us kids north and retired in the state of Washington where he filled his retirement years with home-spun aviaries, kit car projects, painting, remodeling, and even baking on occasion.

On August 28, 1995, although ill, my father escorted my mother to the dance floor as we celebrated their 50th wedding anniversary in Seattle. Slowly swaying to the tunes of *Sentimental Journey*, he held my mother close to him and hid his face. It was the second time I had ever seen my father cry. Two and a half years later my father was again surrounded by family as we said good-bye to him at a care center in Bellevue.

Ivet lived out her life as wife, mother, grandmother, and homemaker—the most loving and selfless human being I have ever met. She was "Mom" to 11 grandchildren, who provided her endless opportunities to satisfy her insatiable need to nurture. At the end of the day, however, it was my father who remained the center of her life. I have been told three times by relatives that a young Tatar girl would never say, "I don't care, I'm going to marry that man." They insist there is no way to translate that into Tatarça—it just wouldn't be said. When my father was dying, my mother and I would visit him in the hospital. She and I would step out, occasionally, for a smoke. She had a cold one day and I scolded her.

"Mom, you shouldn't be smoking with that cold!"

"I don't care," she snapped at me. "I'm going with him."

When it came to being with my father, whether it was an imposing prison fence, the formidable hills of Kobe, incessant air raids, hundreds of years of family tradition, or even the naïve advice of a son, nothing ever stood in her way.

Ivet died of heart failure on her wedding anniversary, August 28, 1999, at her home in Bellevue. We like to think that Ed and Ivet shared their 54th anniversary together.

Ed and Ivet Bacon

CPSIA information can be obtained
at www.ICGtesting.com
Printed in the USA
LVOW10*2027210217
524938LV00017B/346/P